The Reference Shelf®

The European Union

Edited by Norris Smith

Editorial Advisor Lynn M. Messina

The Reference Shelf
Volume 77• Number 1

The H.W. Wilson Company
2005

The Reference Shelf

The books in this series contain reprints of articles, excerpts from books, addresses on current issues, and studies of social trends in the United States and other countries. There are six separately bound numbers in each volume, all of which are usually published in the same calendar year. Numbers one through five are each devoted to a single subject, providing background information and discussion from various points of view and concluding with a subject index and comprehensive bibliography that lists books, pamphlets, and abstracts of additional articles on the subject. The final number of each volume is a collection of recent speeches, and it contains a cumulative speaker index. Books in the series may be purchased individually or on subscription.

Library of Congress has cataloged this title as follows:

The European Union / edited by Norris Smith.
      p. cm. — (The reference shelf; v. 77, no. 1)
      Includes bibliographical references and index.
      ISBN 0-8242-1046-8
      1. European Union. I Smith, Norris. II. Series

JN30.E94 2005
341.242'2'09—dc22

2004062511

On the cover: The flag of the European Union.

Visit H.W. Wilson's Web site: www.hwwilson.com

Printed in the United States of America

Contents

Preface vii

I. History and Structure 1

Editor's Introduction 3
1) The European Union at a Glance. *EUROPA* 5
2) Institutions of the European Union. *Wikipedia* 9
3) Peace in Our Time. Gideon Rachman. *Economist* 17
4) Can the EU Win the Love of Europeans? Graham Bowley.
   International Herald Tribune 22
5) Blair's Support of Closer EU Links Draws Fire. Gregory Katz.
   The Dallas Morning News 25
6) European Union Debates Nod to God in Constitution. Rebecca Goldsmith.
   Religion News Service 28

II. EU Membership 31

Editor's Introduction 33
1) Europe's Big Gamble. Don Belt. *National Geographic* 35
2) EU Expansion Brings Expectations, Fears for New Members. Roger Wilkison.
   Voice of America News 42
3) European Integration Unplugged. Martin Rücker. *Foreign Policy* 45
4) Second-class Allies. John Kampfner. *New Statesman* 50
5) Turks Worry That a Union With Europe Will Cost Them Their Soul.
   Susan Sachs. *The New York Times* 53

III. Trade and Finance 57

Editor's Introduction 59
1) Few Problems in Euro Takeover. David Rising. Associated Press 61
2) Europe's New Members Not Ready for the Euro. Mark Landler.
   The New York Times 63
3) Europe's Society Under Strain, Says Leaked Economic Report.
   Richard Carter. *EUobserver.com* 66
4) Beyond Integration. Michael Deppler. *Finance & Development* 68
5) EU Offers to Eliminate Its Farm Export Subsidies at World Trade Talks,
   But Only If U.S., Canada, Japan Follow. Constant Brand. Associated Press . . . 79
6) Old Continent, New Deal. Martha Neil. *ABA Journal* 81

IV. Open Borders 89

Editor's Introduction 91
1) Containing the Flow. *Canada and the World Backgrounder* 93
2) Melting Pot. Stryker McGuire, et al. *Newsweek*. 96
3) Italy Plays Role of Europe's Immigration Gatekeeper. Sophie Arie.
   The Christian Science Monitor 99
4) Migration and EU Enlargement. *OECD Observer* 101
5) Immigration Could Strain EU Health Services. Colin Meek.
   Canadian Medical Association Journal 103
6) Czech Republic Fears EU Membership Will Lure Doctors. Dinah A. Spritzer.
   Canadian Medical Association Journal 105

V. EU Security and Relations with the U.S. 107

Editor's Introduction 109
1) Commission Proposes Crisis Centre for Terrorist Attacks. Honor Mahony.
   EUobserver 111
2) Military Skills Key to European Influence in U.S. Louis R. Golino.
   The Washington Times 113
3) Europe Takes Charge. Andrew Moravcsik. *Newsweek* 119
4) EU "Must Work with U.S. As an Ally." Toby Helm. *Daily Telegraph* 123
5) A More Perfect Union? Sam Natapoff. *The American Prospect* 125
6) Transatlantic Divides. Wen Stephenson. *Boston Globe* 129

VI. Environmental Policy 133

Editor's Introduction 135
1) Doomsday Climate Warning for EU. Gareth Harding. United Press
   International. 137
2) Emissions Pact Goes Forward. Peter N. Spotts. *The Christian Science Monitor*. . 140
3) Bigger EU Could Affect Environmental Policies. Maria Burke.
   Environmental Science & Technology 143
4) Europe Is United: No Bioengineered Food. Elisabeth Rosenthal.
   International Herald Tribune 147

Appendix: Timeline of the European Union 151

Bibliography 157
Books 159
Web Sites 161
Additional Periodical Articles with Abstracts 163

Index 173

Preface

This book is intended as an introduction to the European Union, a unique conglomeration of nation-states that is playing an increasing role in world affairs. Although "Europe" is often defined as a continent, it is really only the western third of the vast land mass that geographers call Eurasia. A relatively small part of the world, it has had an enormous impact on human history. For centuries its kings and peoples fought each other over territory, trade, and religion; in the modern era, several of its nation-states acquired lands abroad, which made their conflicts global. Europe was both flashpoint and battle-ground in the world wars of the 20th century, which had, by the end of World War II, taken a savage toll on the region's population and destroyed much of its infrastructure, as well as many of its social and political institutions; the last of the European colonial empires had also begun to crumble.

After the war, Europe was effectually divided into rival spheres of influence by the victorious, quasi-European superpowers, with the Soviet Union, which had suffered more during the war, exercising much tighter and far more oppressive control over Eastern Europe than the United States did over the West. It was in Western Europe that the notion of a consensual, pan-European effort to resolve differences and avert future wars first emerged; it also seemed to many Europeans that only as a bloc could they maintain their traditional importance in world affairs.

From small beginnings, as a modest confederation for managing coal and steel, the European Union has grown to encompass 25 nations, approximately 455 million people, and more than 2 million square miles of territory, extending from the Mediterranean to the Arctic Circle and from the Atlantic coast to the borders of Ukraine and Belarus. Its collective economy is currently one of the world's largest, although none of its constituent nations can match the economy of the United States. Earlier attempts at European unification—the empires of the Caesars, Charlemagne, the Hapsburgs, Napoleon, and Hitler—were accomplished through conquest and dynastic ambition; by contrast the EU has been constructed slowly and haltingly through a series of dry, unglamorous treaties focused, as a rule, on specific practical issues, such as fishing quotas or steel tariffs, and punctiliously respectful of the sovereignty of its members. At every step, skeptics have predicted its demise, but bit by bureaucratic bit, the EU has become a power to reckon with in trade and finance, and may in time develop into a full-fledged political entity.

A draft constitution that would restructure the existing network of treaties and agreements and more sharply define the EU's various institutions has been approved by representatives of all the member states; however, since it might involve some encroachments on national sovereignty, at least 11 of the signatory governments intend to submit the constitution to a popular vote as well. It is not clear what will happen over the next few years if any of these referenda fails (aside from considerable embarrassment to national politicians), but the EU is accustomed to slow, persistent negotiations and manifold options, including the occasional "opt-out" clause that allows a nation to decide how far it wishes to follow the Union's policies.

In whatever direction the EU continues to evolve, it has already accomplished more than most people ever expected. It has created a sizable free-trade area and provided the machinery for resolving disputes among sovereign nations, thus keeping the peace, and it has begun to put forward a distinctively European identity—all this in a part of the world where more than 20 languages are spoken and where ethnic fears and national rivalries have a long and sanguinary history. The EU has also played an important—and underappreciated—role in Western Europe's economic and political recovery from World War II, raising standards of living and promoting democratic governments across the board; it now hopes to do the same in Eastern Europe.

The Union's ambitious program of enlargement and consolidation might suggest dreams of becoming a collective superpower, but if such dreams exist, they are still very remote. So far, enlargement has worked to reduce cohesion, and national sovereignty has emerged as an almost nonnegotiable issue. (The proposed new constitution was rejected in 2003 and then revised to restore veto power to the member states in such vital areas as defense and taxation. It is too early to tell whether the rifts and stresses evident within the European Union itself are simply growing pains that will pass as the organization adjusts to its new size and achieves greater coherence, or signs that it is nearing its natural limits and can now only fragment or decline. Although the EU once adopted an anthem (Beethoven's "Ode to Joy"), it has never chosen a totem animal on the lines of the Russian bear or the American eagle—if it did, the animal might well be a colorless, shape-shifting amoeba, or else one of those ancient mythological creatures put together from half a dozen different species.

The most significant failures of the EU have been its apparent paralysis in the face of mass killings in the former Yugoslavia during the 1990s (the United States and NATO finally took action, and the EU is now developing armed forces of its own) and its pervasive inability to win the trust and affection of its own populace. To many Europeans it remains a distant, slightly mad bureaucracy, probably corrupt or secretly controlled by unfriendly powers. This unflattering view has been encouraged by national leaders who find it convenient to blame "Brussels" for every unpopular measure and take credit for anything that works, but the EU has often exacerbated the problem with numbing jargon and lofty "we know best" attitudes. In fact, the Union has done much for Europe's diverse peoples, and the advantages of membership are such that, while states are free to leave, only one (Greenland) ever has, although several have declined to participate in one or another of the Union's activities. The loose structure of the Union and its "work in progress" character make all sorts of adjustments possible, and, of course, open the way to interminable negotiations.

This book is divided into six sections. Part I describes the growth and structure of the Union and some of the problems thrown into high relief by its proposed new constitution, which will be the subject of popular referenda for several years to come. Part II examines the EU's historic expansion in May 2004, when it took in 10 new members at once (eight from the former Soviet Union) and then confirmed plans for future enlargements, including a controversial proposal to accept a Muslim republic. The articles in Part III deal with the EU's activities in trade and finance, where it has had a strong presence almost from the start, while those in Part IV concern the implications of open borders and the free movement of populations for Europe's economy and its treasured social services, as well as the identity crises that migrants can provoke in states that have traditionally defined themselves by ethnicity. Part V deals with European security issues, and particularly with Europe's interest in developing a military force of its own, beyond the older NATO alliance with the United States. Defense is only one of the areas in which European and American interests may ultimately diverge. Another is covered in Part VI, which explores the EU's approach to environmental questions—the Union is the principal supporter of the Kyoto Protocol on global warming, which the United States rejects. Because their economies are linked by international trade, however, American manufacturers may have to take European policies into account whether they agree with them or not. As the EU continues to grow, it may come into conflict with other world powers, more than it has heretofore. In the Appendix which follows the book's six sections, a timeline of significant events in the formation and evolution of the European Union is provided.

Perhaps because the subject is somewhat amorphous, relatively little space has been given to the European Union in the American press, so that assembling this Reference Shelf has been more challenging than usual. I would like to thank the authors and publishers—many of them foreign—of the articles reprinted here for extending their permissions, and my colleagues Lynn Messina, Sandra Watson, Jennifer Peloso, and Rich Stein for unfailing help and encouragement.

Norris Smith
February 2005

I. History and Structure

The Member States of the European Union

- Austria
- Belgium
- Denmark
- Cyprus
- Czech Republic
- Estonia
- Finland
- France
- Germany

- Greece
- Hungary
- Ireland
- Italy
- Luxembourg
- Latvia
- Lithuania
- Malta
- The Netherlands

- Poland
- Portugal
- Slovakia
- Slovenia
- Spain
- Sweden
- United Kingdom

Candidate Countries:
- Bulgaria
- Croatia
- Romania
- Turkey

Application Pending:
- Former Yugoslav Republic of Macedonia

Source: *EUROPA*, the official Web site of the European Union (*europa.eu.int*). Copyright © *EUROPA*, 2004.

Editor's Introduction

The articles in this section concern the basic structure of the European Union and the way it seems to be developing. The first piece, "The European Union at a Glance," from the Union's own *EUROPA* Web site, provides a short overview of the EU's purpose and structure and a somewhat longer account of its history. (For an extended timeline, see the Appendix at the end of this book.) Then, in "The Institutions of the European Union" from the online *Wikipedia*, the European Parliament, Council, Commission, and Court of Justice are described. (The latter should not be confused with the World Court at the Hague—the EU court is strictly for EU business. Its judges are appointed by member states and serve six-year terms.) These two articles give a good idea of the Union's scope and its truly international character, but they do not address the concerns of "euroskeptics," who exist in all the member states. Skepticism is particularly biting right now because the EU seems to be at a turning point, on the verge of becoming much stronger or else falling into decline.

In an evaluation of the past aims and present direction of the European Union entitled "Peace in Our Time" from the *Economist*, Gideon Rachman emphasizes the extent to which Europe and its leaders have been haunted by memories of war—of bloodbaths that seem like ancient history to a younger generation. If a visceral fear of war helped hold the Union together in the 20th century, what will do so in the 21st? Rachman identifies two factions within the EU, with different agendas. One is composed of the West European nations led by France and Germany, who would like to forge a tighter union and demonstrate a clear independence from America in foreign policy. The other is made up of Britain, Italy, Spain, and now some of the new member states from Eastern Europe, who are suspicious of "superstate" ambitions and think the Union should focus on trade and economic development; these nations generally regard the United States as a necessary ally.

The tension between the "Euro-nationalists" and the "Atlanticists," as they are called, is being played out in the bumpy progress of the EU's proposed constitution, which has already been redrafted to reduce central authority and is now also to be subject to a series of plebiscites, where it may very well be rejected. In "Can the EU Win the Love of Europeans?" from the *International Herald Tribune*, Graham Bowley describes the apathy and antagonism that dog the EU at a grassroots level and the EU's belated attempt to repair its image. It is perhaps significant that the European Parliament, the only EU institution whose members are directly elected, is also the weakest of the EU's governing bodies (it can reject or accept legislation proposed by the Commission, but it cannot initiate bills). In fact, the European Union is not a very democratic organization—many feel that its structure reflects an elite distrust of mass movements and popular enthusiasms, a distrust that is certainly reciprocated by the populace. Britons are particularly ambivalent about their country's membership in the EU, as Gregory Katz explains in "Blair's Support of Closer EU Links Draws Fire." Among the concerns of Great Britain's "Euroskeptics" are the possible abandonment of British currency for the euro, as well as the potential need to surrender a modicum of diplomatic, judicial, economic, and military authority to the EU with the adoption of the new constitution.

A side issue that has involved people in many countries concerns the preamble to the proposed constitution. At present, it makes no mention of the Judeo-Christian God or of any supreme being. As Rebecca Goldsmith reports for the Religion News Service in "European Union Debates Nod to God in Constitution," this seems to some a betrayal of Europe's own cultural heritage, while to others, the attempt to introduce religious language into a secular document smacks of bigotry (all parties to this dispute are very much aware of Muslim Turkey's application for membership, which will be discussed in the next section).

The European Union at a Glance

EUROPA, 2004

The European Union (EU) is a family of democratic European countries, committed to working together for peace and prosperity. It is not a state intended to replace existing states, but it is more than any other international organisation. The EU is, in fact, unique. Its member states have set up common institutions to which they delegate some of their sovereignty so that decisions on specific matters of joint interest can be made democratically at a European level. This pooling of sovereignty is also called "European integration."

The historical roots of the European Union lie in the Second World War. The idea of European integration was conceived to prevent such killing and destruction from ever happening again. It was first proposed by the French foreign minister Robert Schuman in a speech on 9 May 1950. This date, the "birthday" of what is now the EU, is celebrated annually as Europe Day.

There are five EU institutions, each playing a specific role:

- European Parliament (elected by the peoples of the member states);
- Council of the European Union (representing the governments of the member states);
- European Commission (driving force and executive body);
- Court of Justice (ensuring compliance with the law);
- Court of Auditors (controlling sound and lawful management of the EU budget).

These are flanked by five other important bodies:

- European Economic and Social Committee (expresses the opinions of organised civil society on economic and social issues);
- Committee of the Regions (expresses the opinions of regional and local authorities);
- European Central Bank (responsible for monetary policy and managing the euro);
- European Ombudsman (deals with citizens' complaints about maladministration by any EU institution or body);

- European Investment Bank (helps achieve EU objectives by financing investment projects).

A number of agencies and other bodies complete the system.

The rule of law is fundamental to the European Union. All EU decisions and procedures are based on the treaties, which are agreed upon by all the EU countries.

Initially, the EU consisted of just six countries: Belgium, Germany, France, Italy, Luxembourg, and the Netherlands. Denmark, Ireland, and the United Kingdom joined in 1973, Greece in 1981, Spain and Portugal in 1986, Austria, Finland, and Sweden in 1995. In 2004 the biggest ever enlargement took place with 10 new countries joining.

In the early years, much of the co-operation between EU countries was about trade and the economy, but now the EU also deals with many other subjects of direct importance for our everyday life, such as citizens' rights; ensuring freedom, security, and justice; job creation; regional development; environmental protection; making globalisation work for everyone.

> *The European Union has delivered half a century of stability, peace, and prosperity.*

The European Union has delivered half a century of stability, peace, and prosperity. It has helped to raise living standards, built a single Europe-wide market, launched the single European currency, the euro, and strengthened Europe's voice in the world.

Unity in diversity: Europe is a continent with many different traditions and languages, but also with shared values. The EU defends these values. It fosters co-operation among the peoples of Europe, promoting unity while preserving diversity and ensuring that decisions are taken as close as possible to the citizens.

In the increasingly interdependent world of the 21st century, it will be even more necessary for every European citizen to co-operate with people from other countries in a spirit of curiosity, tolerance, and solidarity.

Beginnings: War and Peace

For centuries, Europe was the scene of frequent and bloody wars. In the period 1870 to 1945, France and Germany fought each other three times, with terrible loss of life. A number of European leaders became convinced that the only way to secure a lasting peace between their countries was to unite them economically and politically.

So, in 1950, the French foreign minister Robert Schuman proposed integrating the coal and steel industries of Western Europe. As a result, in 1951, the European Coal and Steel Community (ECSC) was set up, with six members: Belgium, West Germany, Luxembourg, France, Italy, and the Netherlands. The power to make decisions about the coal and steel industry in these countries was placed in the hands of an independent, supranational body called the "High Authority." Jean Monnet was its first president.

From Three Communities to the European Union

The ECSC was such a success that, within a few years, these same six countries decided to go further and integrate other sectors of their economies. In 1957 they signed the Treaties of Rome, creating the European Atomic Energy Community (EURATOM) and the European Economic Community (EEC). The member states set about removing trade barriers between them and forming a "common market."

In 1967 the institutions of the three European communities were merged. From this point on, there was a single Commission and a single Council of Ministers as well as the European Parliament.

Originally, the members of the European Parliament were chosen by the national parliaments but in 1979 the first direct elections were held, allowing the citizens of the member states to vote for the candidate of their choice. Since then, direct elections have been held every five years.

The Treaty of Maastricht (1992) introduced new forms of co-operation between the member state governments—for example on defense, and in the area of "justice and home affairs." By adding this inter-governmental co-operation to the existing "Community" system, the Maastricht Treaty created the European Union (EU).

Integration Means Common Policies

Economic and political integration between the member states of the European Union means that these countries have to take joint decisions on many matters. So they have developed common policies in a very wide range of fields—from agriculture to culture, from consumer affairs to competition, from the environment and energy to transport and trade.

In the early days the focus was on a common commercial policy for coal and steel and a common agricultural policy. Other policies were added as time went by, and as the need arose. Some key policy aims have changed in the light of changing circumstances. For example, the aim of the agricultural policy is no longer to produce as much food as cheaply as possible but to support farming methods that produce healthy, high-quality food and protect the environment. The need for environmental protection is now taken into account across the whole range of EU policies.

The European Union's relations with the rest of the world have also become important. The EU negotiates major trade and aid agreements with other countries and is developing a common foreign and security policy.

The Single Market: Banning the Barriers

It took some time for the member states to remove all the barriers to trade between them and to turn their "common market" into a genuine single market in which goods, services, people, and capital could move around freely. The single market was formally completed at the end of 1992, though there is still work to be done in some areas—for example, to create a genuinely single market in financial services.

During the 1990s it became increasingly easy for people to move around in Europe, as passport and customs checks were abolished at most of the EU's internal borders. One consequence is greater mobility for EU citizens. Since 1987, for example, more than a million young Europeans have taken study courses abroad, with support from the EU.

The Single Currency: The Euro in Your Pocket

In 1992 the EU decided to go for economic and monetary union (EMU), involving the introduction of a single European currency managed by a European Central Bank. The single currency—the euro—became a reality on 1 January 2002, when euro notes and coins replaced national currencies in 12 of the 15 countries of the European Union (Belgium, Germany, Greece, Spain, France, Ireland, Italy, Luxembourg, the Netherlands, Austria, Portugal, and Finland).

The Growing Family

The EU has grown in size with successive waves of accessions. Denmark, Ireland, and the United Kingdom joined in 1973 followed by Greece in 1981, Spain and Portugal in 1986 and Austria, Finland, and Sweden in 1995. The European Union welcomed 10 new countries in 2004: Cyprus, the Czech Republic, Estonia, Hungary, Latvia, Lithuania, Malta, Poland, Slovakia, and Slovenia. Bulgaria and Romania expect to follow a few years later and Turkey is also a candidate country. To ensure that the EU can continue functioning efficiently with 25 or more members, its decision-making system must be streamlined. That is why the Treaty of Nice lays down new rules governing the size of the EU institutions and the way they work. It came into force on 1 February 2003.

Institutions of the European Union

WIKIPEDIA, OCTOBER–NOVEMBER 2004

European Parliament

Powers and Competencies

The European Parliament is one half of a bilateral legislature (the other half is the Council of the European Union). It has co-legislative power with the Council in most EU policy areas, able to accept, amend, or reject proposals as it sees fit.

It also has a budgetary function, adopting the final budget of the European Union.

Additionally, Parliament exerts a function of democratic supervision over all the EU's activities, particularly the European Commission, which it has the sole power to elect and dismiss, and calls to account as it sees fit.

Under the proposed new treaty establishing a constitution for Europe, Parliament's powers are enhanced, with a greater degree of democratic scrutiny, the right to co-legislate in virtually all areas of policy, and control over the entire EU budget.

History

The European Coal and Steel Community established a Common Assembly in September 1952, its members drawn from the six national parliaments of the ECSC's constituent nations. This was expanded in March 1958 to also cover the European Economic Community and Euratom. It immediately adopted the name European Parliamentary Assembly, and used the name European Parliament from 1962. In 1979 it was expanded again with its members being directly elected. Thereafter it was simply expanded whenever new nations joined, and the membership was adjusted (upwards) in 1994 after German reunification, until the Treaty of Nice set a cap on membership at 732.

Party Groups in the European Parliament

At the commencement of Parliament's sixth term (2004–2009), there were seven groups, plus Non-Inscrits (non-aligned members). As of July 21, 2004, the composition of the Parliament was:

- EPP-ED (European People's Party [Christian Democrats] and European Democrats): 268 seats

- PSE (Party of European Socialists): 198 seats
- ALDE (Alliance of Liberals and Democrats for Europe) (European Liberal Democrat and Reform Party and European Democratic Party): 88 seats
- Greens-EFA (European Federation of Green Parties/European Free Alliance): 42 seats
- GUE-NGL (European United Left / Nordic Green Left): 41 seats
- IND/DEM (Independence and Democracy): 37 seats
- UEN (Union for a Europe of Nations): 27 seats
- Some of the members of the European Parliament prefer not to belong to any political group. These independent members are referred to as NI (Non-Inscrits): 29 seats

The makeup of Parliament's groups is fairly fluid, and delegations (or indeed individual members) are free to switch allegiances as they see fit.

European Parliament party groups are distinct from the corresponding political parties, although they are intimately linked. Usually, the European parties also have member parties from European countries which are not members of the European Union.

Representation

The European Parliament represents 450 million citizens of the European Union. Since 13 June 2004, there are 732 Members of the European Parliament (MEPs), with a proportionally larger representation for smaller member states. This number was temporarily raised to 788 to accommodate representatives from the 10 states that joined the EU on 1 May 2004, but will remain fixed at 732 even after the accession of Romania and Bulgaria in 2007.

Elections

Elections to the Parliament are held using various forms of proportional representation, as selected by the member states. These forms include regional and national lists and single transferable vote.

The most recent elections were held on 10–13 June 2004. Following the enlargement of the Union on 1 May, they were the largest simultaneous transnational elections ever held in the world, with nearly 400 million citizens eligible to vote.

Council of the European Union

The Council of the European Union forms, along with the European Parliament, the legislative arm of the European Union (EU). It contains ministers of the governments of each of the member-states of the EU. The Council of the European Union is sometimes referred to in official European Union documents simply as the Council, and it is often informally referred to as the Council of Ministers.

Formations of the Council

Legally speaking, the Council is a single entity, but it is in practice divided into several different councils, each dealing with a different functional area. Each council contains a different type of ministers.

There are currently nine formations:

1. **General Affairs and External Relations (or GAERC):** The most important of the formations, it is composed of foreign ministers and meets once a month. Since June 2002 it holds separate meetings on general affairs and external relations.

   - The General Affairs Council also coordinates preparation for and follow-up to meetings of the European Council.

   - At its sessions on external relations, under the context of the Common Foreign and Security Policy, the High Representative for Common Foreign and Security Policy also takes part.

2. **Economic and Financial Affairs (or Ecofin):** Composed of economics and finance ministers of the member states.

3. **Agriculture and Fisheries:** One of the oldest configurations, it brings together once a month the ministers for agriculture and fisheries and the commissioners responsible for agriculture, fisheries, food safety, veterinary questions, and public health matters.

4. **Justice and Home Affairs Council (or JHA):** This configuration brings together justice ministers and interior ministers of the member states.

5. **Employment, Social Policy, Health, and Consumer Affairs Council (or EPSCO):** Composed of employment, social protection, consumer protection, health, and equal opportunities ministers.

6. **Competitiveness:** Created in June 2002 through the merging of three previous configurations (Internal Market, Industry, and Research). Depending on items on the agenda, it is composed of European affairs ministers, industry ministers, research ministers, etc.

7. **Transport, Telecommunications, and Energy:** Again created in June 2002 through the merging of three policies under one configuration, and composition again varying according to the items on the agenda. It meets approximately every two months.

8. **Environment:** Composed of environment ministers who meet about four times a year.

9. **Education, Youth, and Culture (or EYC):** Composed of education, culture, youth, and communication ministers who meet around three or four times a year.

Voting

The Council votes either by unanimity or by qualified majority voting. The voting system used for a given decision depends on the policy area to which that decision belongs; according to the treaties, some subjects require unanimity, while others require only a qualified majority.

Even in those areas which require a qualified majority, the Council is required to try to reach a unanimous decision where possible.

Countries of the EU hold different numbers of votes in the Council. The number of votes held by each country is based indirectly on the size of the country's population, but with proportionally heavier weighting towards smaller countries. This concept is aimed at balancing the voice of big countries with the voice of small countries.

On November 1, 2004, modified voting weights from the Treaty of Nice will come into effect (this date was revised by the Treaty of Accession 2003 from the original intention of January 1, 2005). This treaty also provides for qualified majority votes to require a "double majority" of both population and number of countries.

Further revisions to voting weights are made in the proposed constitutional treaty which was signed on October 29, 2004.

European Commission

The European Commission (formally the Commission of the European Communities) is the executive of the European Union. The Commission is headed by a president (from November 2004, José Durão Barroso of Portugal). Its primary roles are to propose legislation and to carry it out.

The Commission is fully independent, and [commissioners are] not permitted to take instructions from the government of their member state.

Responsibilities of the Commission

The Commission represents the general interest of the Union as a whole. It has sole authority to initiate legislation . . . in most policy areas, though it can be requested to do so by the Council of the European Union or the European Parliament, and it shares the power of initiative with the member states in . . . foreign policy and defense and . . . criminal law.

The Commission is the guardian of the treaties, and is responsible as such for initiating infringement proceedings against member states and others who violate the treaties and other community law.

The Commission negotiates international trade agreements (in the World Trade Organization) and other international agreements on behalf of the Community. It closely co-operates in this with the Council of the European Union.

The Commission is responsible for adopting technical implementing measures to implement legislation adopted by the Council and, in most cases, the Parliament. This legislation is subject to the approval of committees of the member states, through the procedure known as comitology.

The Commission functions as competition regulator for the Union, vetting all mergers with Community-wide effects, and initiating proceedings against companies which violate competition laws.

Appointment and Makeup of the Commission

At present, the Commission consists of 30 commissioners: one from each member state, plus an additional commissioner from each of the five largest member states: France, Germany, Italy, the UK, and Spain. Each commissioner holds a policy portfolio.

The president of the Commission is chosen by the European Council [EU heads of state], a choice which must be approved by the European Parliament. The remaining commissioners are appointed by the member states in agreement with the president. Finally, the new Commission as a whole must be approved by the Parliament.

The European Parliament has the power to force the entire Commission to resign by a vote of no confidence (requiring a vote of two-thirds of those voting and of a majority of the total membership). While it has never used this power, it threatened to use it against the Santer Commission in 1999 whereupon the whole Commission resigned of its own accord.

The number [of commissioners] will be reduced on 1 November 2004 to 25, with one commissioner from each member state. The following proposed list of portfolio holders was announced on August 12 by President-designate José Durão Barroso:

- José Durão Barroso (Portugal), president of the Commission
- Margot Wallström (Sweden), first vice president, Institutional Relations and Communication Strategy
- Jacques Barrot (France), vice president, Transport
- Rocco Buttiglione (Italy), vice president, Justice, Freedom, and Security
- Siim Kallas (Estonia), vice president, Administrative Affairs, Audit, and Anti-Fraud
- Günter Verheugen (Germany), vice president, Enterprise and Industry
- Joaquín Almunia (Spain), Economic & Monetary Affairs

- Joe Borg (Malta), Fisheries and Maritime Affairs
- Stavros Dimas (Greece), Environment
- Dalia Grybauskaite (Lithuania), Financial Programming and Budget
- Benita Ferrero-Waldner (Austria), External Relations and European Neighbourhood Policy
- Jan Figel (Slovakia), Education, Training, Culture, and Multilingualism
- Mariann Fischer Boel (Denmark), Agriculture and Rural Development
- Danuta Hübner (Poland), Regional Policy
- László Kovács (Hungary), Energy
- Neelie Kroes (Netherlands), Competition
- Marcos Kyprianou (Cyprus), Health and Consumer Protection
- Charlie McCreevy (Ireland), Internal Market and Services
- Peter Mandelson (United Kingdom), Trade
- Louis Michel (Belgium), Development and Humanitarian Aid
- Janez Potočnik (Slovenia), Science and Research
- Viviane Reding (Luxembourg), Information Society and Media
- Olli Rehn (Finland), Enlargement
- Vladimír Špidla (Czech Republic), Employment, Social Affairs, and Equal Opportunities
- Ingrida Udre (Latvia), Taxation and Customs Union

Hearings before the committees of the European Parliament questioned the suitability of several of the candidates; a full-scale row broke out over Rocco Buttiglione's reported views on homosexuality and women, and the committees also found fault with

- László Kovács for insufficient professional competence in the energy field;
- Neelie Kroes for insufficient detailed grasp of certain specific subjects;
- Mariann Fischer-Boel for insufficient determination to defend European farmers' interests, and an unwillingness to enter into a dialogue with the Parliament;
- and noted that Ingrida Udre faced allegations of irregularities in the funding of her political party.

On October 27, 2004, José Durão Barroso withdrew his proposal for the new Commission to prevent it from probable rejection by the European Parliament. Romani Prodi's team remain in office in a caretaker capacity. On November 4, Mr. Barroso announced the following changes to his proposed team:

- Franco Frattini (Italy), vice-president, Justice, Freedom, and Security
- László Kovács (Hungary), Taxation and Customs Union
- Andris Piebalgs (Latvia), Energy.

History

The Commission originated in the High Authority of the European Coal and Steel Community, which was established in 1952 under the terms of the Treaty Establishing the European Coal and Steel Community. Later in 1958 the Commission of the European Economic Community and the Commission of the European Atomic Energy Community were established under the terms of the Treaties of Rome. Finally, in 1967, these three bodies merged to form the Commission of the European Communities, established under the terms of the Merger Treaty. This is the body that continues to exist to this day.

European Court of Justice

The European Court of Justice (ECJ) is the 'Court of Justice of the European Communities,' i.e. the court of the European Union (EU). It is based in Luxembourg, unlike most of the rest of the European Union governance, which is based in Brussels and Strasbourg.

The ECJ is the supreme court of the European Union. It adjudicates on matters of interpretation of European law, most commonly:

- Claims by the European Commission that a member state has not implemented a European Union Directive or other legal requirement.

- Claims by member states that the European Commission has exceeded its authority.

- References from national courts in the EU member states asking the ECJ what a particular piece of EC law means. The Union has many languages and competing political interests, and so local courts often have difficulty deciding what a particular piece of legislation means in any given context. The ECJ will give its opinion, which may or may not clarify the point, and return the case to the national court to be disposed of. The ECJ is only permitted to aid in interpretation of the law, not decide the facts of the case itself.

Individuals cannot bring cases to the ECJ. Employees of the European Commission and related EU bodies used to be able to sue their employer in the ECJ. However, there is now a lower court called the Court of First Instance which deals with these cases.

The ECJ is frequently confused with the European Court of Human Rights, which is based in Strasbourg. However, while the ECJ is part of the European Union, the European Court of Human Rights is not.

The European Parliament is the parliamentary body of the European Union. Other organisations of European countries such as NATO, the OSCE, the Council of Europe, and the Western European Union have parliamentary assemblies as well, but the European Parliament is unique in that it is directly elected by the people and has legislative power. The members of the parliamentary assemblies of the OSCE, the Council of Europe, and the Western European Union are appointed by national parliaments.

Peace in Our Time

By Gideon Rachman
Economist, September 25, 2004

In the whole of Europe there is probably no more blood-soaked battlefield than Verdun. In 1916 some 800,000 French and German soldiers were killed or wounded, fighting inconclusively over a few square miles of territory near the Franco-German border. The young Charles de Gaulle was wounded three times and captured at Verdun. Louis Delors, a 21-year-old French private, suffered terrible injuries there and was almost killed by a German officer who was finishing off the French wounded with a pistol. In the 1990s his son, Jacques Delors, became the founding father of a monetary union of France, Germany, and ten other European countries. Mr. Delors's two great collaborators were Helmut Kohl, the German chancellor, whose father had also fought at Verdun, and François Mitterrand, the French president. In 1984 these two leaders, in a historic act of Franco-German reconciliation, walked hand in hand across the battlefield that had been a killing ground for so many young men from both countries.

Many of the European Union's most ardent supporters still see the EU as a crucial bulwark against the return of war to Europe. In pressing the case for monetary union, Mr. Kohl argued that adopting the euro was ultimately a question of war and peace in Europe. When efforts to write a European constitution looked like stalling, Elmar Brok, a prominent German member of the EU's constitutional convention (and confidant of Mr. Kohl), gave warning that if Europe failed to agree on a constitution, it risked sliding back into the kind of national rivalries that had led to the outbreak of the First World War.

Remember the Bad Old Days?

Such arguments resonate particularly strongly among an older generation of French and German politicians, but also have wider currency. Timothy Garton Ash of St. Antony's College, Oxford, one of Britain's most astute observers of European affairs, says in a recent book that the Union is needed "to prevent us falling back into the bad old ways of war and European barbarism which stalked the Balkans into the very last year of the last century." Mr. Garton Ash concedes that "we can never prove that a continent-wide collection of independent, fully sovereign European democracies would not behave in the same broadly pacific way without the existence of any European Union. Maybe they would, but would you care to risk it?"

Believers in the pacifying effects of the drive for European unity acknowledge the contributions to peace in post-war Europe made by American troops and by the spread of prosperity and democracy. But they argue that the EU has played the central role, by forcing European leaders to co-operate intensively and continuously, by proving that membership of the Union brings prosperity and by demanding that all EU countries adhere to basic principles of democracy, human rights, and the peaceful resolution of disputes.

Seen in this light, EU enlargement is part of the same "peace project" that was initially centred on reconciliation between France and Germany. Countries that apply to join the EU first have to meet a set of basic democratic criteria, and have to put aside old territorial disputes. Eight former members of the Soviet block were admitted to the EU this year, and Romania and Bulgaria are lined up for entry in 2007. But the idea that enlargement of the European Union

---

> ### *EU enlargement is part of the same "peace project" that was initially centred on reconciliation between France and Germany.*

---

will inevitably resolve conflicts and spread freedom and democracy will face even bigger tests in future.

The European Commission in Brussels has already made it clear that all the Balkan countries are potentially eligible for membership, in the hope of encouraging them to make peace and introduce democratic reforms. Croatia, which earlier this year became the first major combatant in the Balkan wars to be formally accepted as a candidate for EU membership, had to step up its co-operation with the International War Crimes Tribunal in The Hague before negotiations became possible.

The EU was rightly castigated for its inability to prevent war in the Balkans in the 1990s, and many Europeans felt humiliated by the need for American military intervention to end the conflicts in Bosnia and Kosovo. But the EU is taking over the peacekeeping mission in Bosnia from NATO later this year in what will be the Union's biggest ever military operation. In the longer term, it is hoped, the prospect of EU membership may help to cement the fragile democracies and the peace settlements now in place across the Balkans.

An Ever Wider Union

A similarly ambitious logic is being applied to Turkey's aspirations to join the Union. Although many EU politicians and citizens are worried about admitting a large Muslim nation into the Union, the proponents of Turkish membership have the upper hand. Turkey is likely to be invited to start negotiations to join the EU later this year. Once again, the key arguments are about peace and the spread of freedom and democracy.

At a time when relations between the West and the Islamic world are so delicate, most EU leaders seem to feel that refusing to admit a large Islamic country into the Union would be seen as a disastrous confirmation of the "clash of civilisations." European diplomats, for their part, hope that admitting Turkey to the EU will bring confirmation that Islam is not incompatible with western values. They point out with some pride that the prospect of EU membership has already driven forward reforms in Turkey such as increased political and civil rights for the Kurdish minority and the abolition of the death penalty.

European diplomats . . . hope that admitting Turkey to the EU will bring confirmation that Islam is not incompatible with western values.

For geo-strategic thinkers sitting in foreign ministries in London, Paris, and Berlin, the arguments for using the EU to spread peace and democratic stability seem compelling. But ordinary European citizens find them much less convincing. Many fear that rather than exporting stability, the EU will import instability. In western Europe, public debate about EU enlargement has tended to concentrate on fears about competition from low-cost labour and waves of immigration. So far such fears have proved containable, and the admission of the new members from central Europe has not caused too much of a fuss. But the new central European members, though poorer than the European average, are smallish (except for Poland), and all are predominantly Christian.

Turkey, which on current trends will have a larger population than any current EU member by 2020, is a different proposition. Because all EU citizens are free to live and work anywhere in the EU, there could be serious resistance to Turkish membership in France, Germany, and the Netherlands, where the rapid growth of Muslim populations in the past 30 years is already a highly sensitive issue.

Even without such worries, the traditional arguments for European integration as a "peace project" have anyway been losing force with the passing years. The current generation of EU leaders still has some memories of the depredations of war in Europe. Gerhard Schröder, the German chancellor, never knew his father, who was killed in the Second World War; Jacques Chirac, the French president, lived through the war as a child. But for most younger Europeans, the threat of war in western Europe now seems almost unimaginably remote.

The expansion of the EU beyond the original six also added new countries with different historical experiences. Although some Britons, such as Mr. Garton Ash, take the threat of a recurrence of war in Europe seriously, the British have generally approached the Union in a very different spirit from the French and Germans. Whereas statesmen such as Monnet and Schuman considered the 1939–45 war as the final proof that traditional European political structures needed to be radically changed, the British tended to see it as a vindication of their own long-established democracy and as confirmation of their anti-continental prejudices. As Margaret Thatcher, a famously Euroskeptic British prime minister, remarked: "In my lifetime all our problems have come from mainland Europe and all the solutions from the English-speaking nations across the world." The British are wary of dreams for political union in Europe. Unlike their French and German counterparts, British politicians have always wanted the EU to be above all about free trade.

Changing the Mix

As the EU has expanded, so Britain has become less isolated in its resistance to the idea that European unity is essential for the maintenance of peace. When in 2003 Sweden held a referendum on whether to join the euro, Goran Persson, the Swedish prime minister, used the peace argument, but watched it fall flat in a neutral country that has been at peace for nearly 200 years. The Swedes voted "no." The new EU members in central Europe also bring a different perspective to the European Union. Whereas the traditional "builders of Europe" were suspicious of nationalism and keen to build up supranational institutions at the expense of the nation-state, many of the central Europeans are still joyfully re-asserting their own national identities after decades of Soviet domination.

Nonetheless, all these countries were eager to join the EU. They saw membership as an assertion of their European identity, as well as a ticket to prosperity and some protection against any threat from a resurgent Russia. But they are also much less enthusiastic than western European federalists about an "ever closer union" for Europe as spelled out in the Treaty of Rome. Vaclav Havel, the hero of the Velvet Revolution and former president of the Czech Republic, explains that for countries that have recently thrown off Soviet domination, "the concept of national sovereignty is something inviolable."

For a variety of reasons, then, the most powerful traditional argument for European unity, peace, has been losing force. European federalists are beginning to look for new rationales for European unity.

Can the EU Win the
Love of Europeans?

By Graham Bowley
International Herald Tribune, October 23, 2004

One afternoon this week, Jeffrey Titford, who has a Union Jack flag on a pole in his garden, stared out to sea and blamed the European Union for most things that have gone wrong in recent years in this frayed tourist town [Frinton-on-Sea] on England's east coast.

EU quotas let French trawlers decimate the local fish stocks, said Titford, 70, who wears a silver lapel badge in the shape of the symbol for the pound sterling. Brussels' regulations had killed British car- and shipbuilding, not to mention agriculture, he said, and were generally shackling the life force of the great British entrepreneurial spirit.

"It seems totally wrong that a country that has been in existence for 1,000 years should have its laws and regulations imposed on it by politicians from other countries," said Titford, who retired as an undertaker in 1989. He joined the UK Independence Party and since then has dedicated himself to the party's cause of withdrawing Britain from the EU.

An observer might have expected that Frinton's proximity to Europe—the Dutch coast lies only a few hours by ferry directly east, and container ships from the Hook of Holland rake the horizon on their way to nearby Harwich—would have bred an enthusiasm for things continental. But in elections to the European Parliament in June, fewer than 4 in 10 people in the Frinton region bothered to turn out for the polls.

And of those who did, 19.6 percent voted for Titford's EU-bashing UK Independence Party

The apathy and plunging popularity of the European Union in places like Frinton is causing the people who run the European Commission in Brussels to rethink the image of the EU. On Nov. 1, when a new college of commissioners under the president-designate, José Manuel Barroso of Portugal, is due to take office, the commission will begin an unprecedented public relations drive to win back apathetic voters and counter skeptics like Titford.

This is a break from the past, when the commission would deliver its dry edicts from on high. Barroso and his colleagues have realized they need a strong voice at the center spelling out the benefits of the European club to member states.

The EU may, in reality, be the defining element of most national politics—and politicians spend weeks each month in Brussels meetings—but they rarely speak out in its favor because it is so unpopular among voters. Instead, they use it as an easy scapegoat for local failings.

Now there could not be more at stake. Europe is due to take another step toward

> *The EU may, in reality, be the defining element of most national politics.*

political integration with the adoption by EU member states of a new constitutional treaty, probably in 2006.

The constitution strengthens the EU's reach into areas such as immigration and criminal law; critics view it as another attack on the independent power of the nation-state in favor of a federal Europe. It is so politically controversial that 11 countries have promised to put its adoption to a referendum.

This includes Britain, but also nations at the heart of Europe like France and the Netherlands. If Barroso does not win the new public relations battle and the experience of last summer's European elections is repeated, then a "no" in these referendums could stop the EU project in its tracks or even lead to its unraveling.

Barroso has appointed Margot Wallstrom, a former Swedish Social Democrat politician, as the EU's first communications commissioner. Her job is to rid the EU of its image of men in suits in office blocks in Brussels, and instead bring a new character and personality to the European project.

In the great push and pull of forces between nations in Europe, the commission hopes that better public relations from Wallstrom will prevent the EU from coming apart.

"We need to explain what exactly it is we do," Wallstrom said in an interview with a handful of reporters in her fourth floor office in Brussels earlier this month.

Wallstrom was a minister of culture and of social affairs in Sweden, and for the last five years held the environment portfolio in the European Commission. Even her most ardent euroskeptic opponents admit hers is a clever appointment as the new communications commissioner. She is a vice president, which means she could run the commission in Barroso's absence. She is a left-leaning leader from northern Europe, which balances Barroso, a former right-of-center Portuguese prime minister.

Wallstrom said that from now on, professional public relations will influence every step of Brussels' policy making.

"We want to reach out," she said. "We will use images and faces of real people who can explain in language that is not full of Eurojargon. There are so many problems that can't be solved by the nation-state. We have not been good at saying that."

But perhaps the most intriguing aspect of Wallstrom's project is her plan to build a "common European narrative." She is still vague on what this means, but she seems to want to create a story about Europe that will give meaning to the EU project. Since stories are one of the chief ways people understand the world, this may be the key to whether Europeans can learn to love the EU—or not. The trouble for Wallstrom is that every nationality has a different story about the EU, and for many the narrative is now turning negative.

"We have no common people, no common feelings," says Jens-Peter Bonde, leader of the euroskeptic group in the European Parliament.

For Jeffrey Titford, who keeps a picture of Winston Churchill in his bathroom, the EU's meaning is clear: it began after the Second World War as a useful form of cooperation and trade, but it has grown into a socialist superstate, run by national elites against the will of the people.

"It was done by the French for French benefit," he says. The only happy ending he desires is a free Britain that returns to the embrace of its former commonwealth.

The European narrative is turning sour not just for die-hard romantics for the British Empire, but for other nations too. Germans cleaved to the EU as a new source of identity as they rebuilt their country after the devastation of the Second World War. But optimism has turned to resentment that Germany continues to be the EU's chief paymaster, subsidizing poorer countries, even as EU rules such as the Stability and Growth Pact stifle its economic growth.

The French are concerned that their power is dwindling in an institution that was meant, they were told, to form Europe in France's image.

The disillusionment has fed into the polls. In the most recent Eurobarometer, only 43 percent of EU citizens said they had a positive image of the union, against 21 percent who had a negative image.

"I don't envy Margot Wallstrom," said Titford, sitting back in his mock-Tudor villa in the quiet avenues of Frinton. "What she's trying to sell is unsellable."

Blair's Support of Closer EU Links Draws Fire

By Gregory Katz
The Dallas Morning News, June 22, 2003

Prime Minister Tony Blair, his popularity suffering a hangover from the Iraq war, is being dragged down by the British public's ambivalent attitude toward forming closer bonds with Europe.

On a number of key questions, Mr. Blair has been hit by critics who say that Britain is giving up its independence in order to fit into the European Union, which holds powerhouses like Germany and France but will soon include far smaller, less consequential countries like Lithuania.

At stake is the future of the British currency, which may be abandoned in favor of the euro already in use on the continent, and Britain's control of its foreign policy, military strategy, and taxation if a proposed EU constitution is adopted by member states.

The fear among "Euroskeptic" Britons, who make up a big part of the population, is that the EU constitution now being drafted will create a European "super state," complete with a powerful president and foreign minister who will speak for all member nations.

Sir Malcolm Rifkind, a former foreign minister from the Conservative Party, said there is little doubt that the trend is toward establishment of a unified super state that would usurp some of Britain's ability to go its own way.

"If you were to create a single currency, a single foreign policy, a single market, a single defense policy, I would say if it walks like a duck and talks like a duck and looks like a duck, it becomes a duck," Mr. Rifkind said.

"I don't say all is lost, that we are actually submerged in a super state already, but many times we've had to change policy—on legal matters, on agriculture, on trade—so we don't have total independence of action anymore."

He said many European national leaders have decided it is acceptable to give up aspects of sovereignty in exchange for tighter political union, which could also amplify Europe's influence. But this view, he said, does not prevail in Britain, even among supporters of closer integration.

"There is a basic gut feeling that we should only concede the loss of sovereignty as little as is unavoidable," Mr. Rifkind said. "Virtually no one is calling for a United States of Europe. There is no enthusiasm for that. The debate is where to draw that line."

> *"Virtually no one is calling for a United States of Europe."*—Sir **Malcolm Rifkind**

Unity Not Ubiquitous

The idea of forging closer ties is simply that Europe, with its strong, diverse economies and large population, can have far more clout if its nations act in unison. But the reality can be quite different, as shown by the divergent views to the Iraq war taken by supporters Britain and Spain, on the one hand, and vocal opponents France and Germany on the other.

Many Britons favor tying Britain closer to the European Union if the EU is treated as a partnership of independent nations, but support for the EU drops dramatically if it is to have the authority to dictate policy to member nations.

These are emotional issues. Uncertainty about Mr. Blair's plan to eventually adopt the euro if economic conditions warrant it, and concerns about sovereignty whipped up by media mogul Rupert Murdoch's tabloid newspapers, have contributed to a fall in Mr. Blair's popularity.

Mr. Blair has also been stung by parliamentary inquiries into his government's use of suspect intelligence reports to convince the British public that an imminent threat from Iraq made war necessary. The prime minister has also been criticized for imposing constitutional changes without consulting the public and Parliament.

As a result of these concerns, the opposition Conservative Party has crept to within four points of Mr. Blair's Labor Party in recent polls, despite the successful campaign to oust Saddam Hussein. In recent years Labor has usually enjoyed a 20- to 30-point survey lead.

The newly emboldened Conservative Party leadership, capitalizing on anti-Europe sentiments, has released 17 "tests" for the proposed EU constitution that must be met before Britain can endorse it. Under the conservatives' plan, the document would be rejected if it calls for EU laws to take precedence over British laws or establishes the post of EU president.

Timid Support

Professor Anand Menon, director of the European Research Institute at the University of Birmingham in England, said the "Euroskeptic" lobby now has the upper hand because the pro-European politicians, including Mr. Blair, have been too timid to make their case effectively.

He said that Mr. Blair has raised expectations that his government will take concrete steps toward more integration with Europe but has backed down.

"British voters are very skeptical about the EU because they don't know any better," he said. "The pro-European governments have been too gutless to talk about it. Blair talks a good game about being part of Europe, but he's not that different from the government before him. He's not doing anything the Conservative Party couldn't have done."

Mr. Blair, who generally favors closer links to Europe, must be extremely careful with regard to European policy because public opinion is sharply divided, said Patrick Dunleavy, a political analyst at the London School of Economics.

"There is not a lot of clarity," he said. "One third of the people have a strong opposition stand, like the Conservative Party does, and 20 to 25 percent of the people, usually the more educated, are very pro-Europe. In between, about half the voters are pretty fluid."

He said the anti-Europe mood often gets whipped up by screaming headlines in Britain's popular and influential tabloids, which far outsell broadsheet newspapers. "It doesn't tend to be well-argued; it tends to be done on a gut level," he said.

A recent example was the front-page headline in *The Sun*—Britain's largest-selling daily—describing the proposed EU constitution as "The Biggest Betrayal in Our History." But many aspects of the constitutional draft have also drawn fire from more thoughtful critics in the more serious newspapers.

Mr. Dunleavy said that many Britons are wary of closer relations with the rest of Europe because of an experience in the early 1990s when Britain was forced out of the European Exchange Rate Mechanism, causing a sharp drop in the value of British currency and a steep rise in national interest rates.

In addition, he said, Britons' attitudes have been shaped by the colonial era, when Britain controlled large portions of the globe unilaterally and did not have to form alliances with countries like France and Germany.

"Brits grew up thinking of themselves as a global player on their own," he said. "Even though that collapsed very quickly, that process of de-colonialization has never really been absorbed. These are cultural attitudes inherited from their parents, and it changes quite slowly."

This worldview was best summed up by a famous newspaper headline from the 1920s. At the time, severe fog hampered visibility in the English Channel, bringing a halt to the vital shipping that linked England to France and the rest of Europe.

"Fog in Channel, Continent Cut Off," said the headline, even though in reality it was Britain, relatively small and perhaps already in decline, that was cut off from the vast population centers of mainland Europe.

European Union Debates Nod to God in Constitution

By Rebecca Goldsmith
Religion News Service, 2004

In France, where most people are Christian but secularism is sacrosanct, the government is battling its burgeoning Muslim population of 5 million over a proposed ban on overt displays of religious devotion.

In Poland, where Catholicism prevails, religious law holds a firm grip on the civil realm.

In Turkey, a secular state made up primarily of Muslims, officials hope to join a European Union that is devoid of explicit references to a Christian God.

As the European Union moves forward with long-term plans to broaden its membership, its leaders are struggling to encompass more ethnicities and religions under one banner than at any time since the Roman Empire.

One of the most heated arguments in the effort to create a pan-European constitution centers on whether it should mention God or religion in its preamble. Talks meant to complete the constitution stalled last month over a disagreement on how much voting power each country would hold.

"We are seeing the tectonic plates of the world's three major religions rubbing up against each other and shooting up sparks," said Graham Watson, the European parliamentary leader of the European Liberal, Democrat, and Reform Party.

"Europe was founded to stop rival tribes from feuding and ethnic cleansing leading to war; we've got to remain vigilant on these issues," Watson said in an interview in Strasbourg, home of the European Union Parliament.

Disagreements pitting religious beliefs against secular values—affecting issues ranging from stem cell research and abortion to freedom of expression—are likely to multiply as the 15-nation European Union prepares to accept 10 more countries in May, growing in representation from 370 million people to 450 million.

The constitutional project, years in the making, is meant to simplify European Union law, which consists of a complex series of disparate treaties, and lay out the Union's shared beliefs and values.

Meeting at the European Union Parliament last month for the final session of the year, both sides of the religion debate put forth their positions.

One camp contended Europe's Christian heritage provides it with common cultural underpinnings, and that ignoring religion would rob a unified Europe of its soul.

Leading the argument are the Poles—devout Catholics now that Communism no longer dictates daily decisions—with support in Catholic countries such as Italy, Spain, and Ireland, as well as from Christian Democratic parties across the continent. In addition, Pope John Paul II has lobbied for a clear reference to God and to the Christian faith.

"The preamble should not divide, it should join Europe," said Edmund Wittbrodt, a Polish observer appointed to the parliament in the year before Poland officially joins the European Union.

"I think the best solution is openness like it is seen by Pope John Paul II. He shows that different religions can get along together.

> *"I thought we had agreed 250 years ago with Montesquieu and Jefferson that a separation between church and state was one of the fundamentals of democracy."*—
> **Graham Watson, European Parliament**

That's the only solution for Europe and the whole world," Wittbrodt said.

On the other side are adherents of the idea of a secular, humanist Europe.

"I thought we had agreed 250 years ago with Montesquieu and Jefferson that a separation between church and state was one of the fundamentals of democracy," said Watson, tying Britain's position to the French political philosopher and the writer of the Declaration of Independence.

The French, in particular, are set against mention of religion in the constitution. They defend their hard-won separation between church and state, which they view as part of their national identity, solidified by a 1905 law created after a struggle against the powerful Catholic Church.

The European Union slogan, "Unity through diversity," rings true for Watson. While he holds Christian beliefs and recognizes the importance of religion in society, he says, he opposes mentioning God in the preamble because it could alienate some Europeans.

"Europe was created by people of different faiths," he said, adding, "A reference to God or a Judeo-Christian God would appear to us to be too limited."

Maurizio Turco, an Italian parliamentary minister, says the inclusion of God is immoral and represents the Catholic Church's attempt to "lock the door against Turkey."

"The main problem is that the Catholic Church wants to impose its morality on everyone," he said, adding, "The main point of religions is that they want to lobby the states to make religious sins into crimes."

At the crux of the debate is the question of how to incorporate Muslims. Growing groups of Muslims live in many of the member countries, and their absorption has proven problematic at times. In France, for instance, Muslim girls' practice of wearing head scarves to school offends the French interpretation of the separation between personal observance and civic secularism.

The Muslim portion of Europe's population, now estimated at 6 percent, would increase dramatically with the addition of Turkey and some of the Balkan states. To some European nationalists, that threatens a demographic upheaval, especially in Christian countries where fertility rates are flagging.

Turkey's candidacy is expected to come up for review this summer. Opponents could seek to plant Christianity in the constitution as a way to discourage Muslims from wanting to join the European Union, Watson said.

That might satisfy German Christian Democrats, for instance, who worry that European family reunification policies would allow Muslim immigrants to flood Germany, overwhelming the native-born population.

Italian Prime Minister Silvio Berlusconi, who held the six-month rotating position of European Union president until Thursday, when Italy passed the baton to the Irish, warned European Parliament members here last month to beware of fundamentalist Muslims who, he said, refuse to fit in with the rest of Europe.

"It becomes clear every time that there is an Arab minority who sees challenge and conflict as something that cannot be avoided," Berlusconi said. "I think it's terrible if we follow that road."

Lennart Sacredeus, a Swedish Christian Democrat and representative to the European Parliament who is deeply religious, said Turkey should be willing to accept Europe's Christian heritage as a requirement to joining the union.

"It is important to mention religion because religion is part of society, and it is part of the lives and values of so many people," said Sacredeus, who adopted a surname meaning "sacred God."

As for Turkey, he said: "It's up to them if they're interested in joining the Union. If their ambition to enter the European Union is for it to not be a Christian club, I think they have the wrong attitude about joining the European Union."

But Richard Corbett, a British socialist who helped write the constitutional draft, wants to offer a more inclusive Europe for new members: "It's a bit late to suddenly turn around and say they're not really European because they have a different religion."

II. EU Membership

Editor's Introduction

In May 2004, after years of preparation, the European Union accepted 10 new members: eight former Soviet states from the Baltic coast and Eastern Europe (Estonia, Latvia, Lithuania, the Czech Republic, Hungary, Poland, Slovakia, and Slovenia) and two Mediterranean island nations (Malta and Greek Cyprus; Turkish Cyprus remains unabsorbed). This was the largest single expansion of the Union ever, and meant significant changes both to the new member states and to the Union itself.

In "Europe's Big Gamble" from *National Geographic*, Don Belt describes the excitement and anxiety coursing through Eastern Europe on the eve of accession. The efforts of the candidate nations to catch up with EU requirements and profit from access to a broader market are then discussed by Roger Wilkison in "EU Expansion Brings Expectations, Fears for New Members," from *Voice of America News*, while in "European Integration Unplugged," from the journal *Foreign Policy*, Martin Rucker examines the bizarre history of a small Lithuanian city whose mammoth electric plant, belching smoke and sulfur dioxide, was closed down by the Communist authorities in favor of nuclear power but is now being reopened and retrofitted for environmental correctness under the auspices of the European Union.

Not all stories have such hopeful endings: In "Second-class Allies," John Kampfner of the *New Statesman* analyzes a pervasive sense of let-down in the new member states as the cost of complying with EU directives begins to be felt and unexpected restrictions on immigration to the West add insult to injury. Nevertheless, none of the new member states has changed its mind and withdrawn from the Union, and two more East European countries—Bulgaria and Romania, both former Stalinist dictatorships—are waiting in the wings.

Also anticipating membership is the republic of Turkey, already a member of NATO and eager to join the European Union. With the acceptance of its application in December 2004, it begins a 10-year transition toward membership, a prospect that is causing considerable uneasiness in parts of Europe and even in Turkey itself, as Susan Sachs reports in "Turks Worry That a Union With Europe Will Cost Them Their Souls" from the *New York Times*. Turkey is a large and populous nation; it is very poor, and it borders on the troubled Middle East. It is barely part of Europe in geographic terms, and to many it seems even less "European" in its culture, which derives from the Islamic rather than the Christian tradition. Opposition to Turkish membership is strongest in those European states that already have substantial, poorly assimilated Muslim minorities: France, Germany, Austria, and the Netherlands. There politicians who support the admission of Turkey may pay a price at the polls. Within Turkey, most people support EU membership for economic reasons, but anti-EU feeling can be strong among religious conservatives and among nationalists who fear that recognition of Kurdish rights will ultimately lead to an independent Kurdistan. The EU, of course, demands guarantees of minority rights; it is also likely to insist that the influence of Turkey's resolutely secular military on the government be curtailed. Although up to now, all nations who have successfully applied to join the EU have eventually been invited to become full-fledged members, the situation with Turkey is sufficiently volatile that the outcome is hard to predict, since the supporters of membership could lose power before negotiations are completed. As always, questions of EU membership are entangled with local issues. No matter how the Turkish question is resolved in the future, the European Union is already changing, as it adjusts to its 10 new members.

Europe's Big Gamble

By Don Belt
National Geographic, May 2004

Stanislaw Nowak wasn't much of a communist. In the 1980s Nowak, a young fruit grower in the hilly Małopolska region of southern Poland, was unhappy with the price that the state-run collective was paying for apples, pears, and plums. But while other farmers were grumbling like good Polish communists, Nowak was cramming two tons of fruit into his one-ton truck and setting out over bad roads to distant cities—Warsaw, Poznań, Gdańsk—to sell on the black market. He traveled alone, squeezed in between bushel baskets with barely enough room to turn the steering wheel. If the police stopped him, he'd plead poverty and tiny mouths to feed, and send them home with an armload of fruit.

When communism crumbled in 1989, leaving many Eastern-bloc farmers to ponder their fate around the kitchen table, Nowak invested his savings in a larger truck, planted more trees, and began marketing dried fruit and bottles of homemade *sliwowica,* a brandy made from plums. And in 1994, when Poland applied to join the European Union (EU), Nowak, like everyone else, joked about clueless Eurocrats who don't know a sheep from a sheepdog, but he also started planning ahead. "No matter what system you live under, you always have to work hard," Nowak, now 43, explains. "But you also have to think. And sometimes you have to take risks."

There's a word in Polish, *sprytny,* that describes Nowak's mentality—a playful, combative, opportunistic state of mind, which has helped the Poles survive one invasion after another for the past thousand years. The most recent—Soviet-imposed communism— set out to obliterate sprytny from the face of the Earth, using terror as an instrument of persuasion. Even in populations as resilient as the Poles, the fear it dispersed took a toll on the minds of ordinary people, like a toxic mist in the air that settles over a town and enters the collective bloodstream, rendering its people passive and lethargic.

Eight of the ten countries joining the European Union this month—Estonia, Latvia, Lithuania, Poland, the Czech Republic, Slovakia, Hungary, and Slovenia—ingested that poison for 50 years, which makes their decision to engage the freewheeling capitalists of Europe all the more audacious. To succeed, they'll need to

---

Crossing (Out) Borders

Complete freedom of movement will phase in gradually. EU citizens can travel anywhere in the bloc but must still show an ID when crossing borders between old and new members, like the one dividing Germany and the Czech Republic. Within a few years such trips should be as easy as passing between U.S. states. But first the EU insists new members tighten their non-EU borders—the Union's frontiers—against illegal immigration and smuggling. A new EU law will allow longtime foreign workers to stay indefinitely—a boon to Cyprus, which relies on imported labor.

---

get communism out of their system, and quickly. But as a taxi driver in Kraków put it, "We were sick for 50 years. It's going to take some time for the symptoms to disappear."

The European Union wasn't meant to heal the sick; it was designed to create wealth. Founded in 1951 as a trade alliance, the EU has grown cautiously, from a cozy group of six at the beginning to 15 member states in 1995, all of them in Western Europe. By integrating their economies and lowering tariffs, these countries created a common market for goods and services, achieving unprecedented levels of prosperity. They also raised the standard of living in poorer EU regions through development grants and subsidies, along with the demand for resources and cheap labor. Today Europe Inc., headquartered in Brussels, is poised to become a global behemoth—a market of 455 million people with a combined GDP of 10 trillion dollars, making it second only to the United States as a political and economic superpower.

Even so, the prospect of adding 10 new countries, 74 million people, and 280,000 square miles to the EU all at once strikes some current members as a reckless gamble—especially since the newcomers were commonly referred to, not long ago, as the basket cases of Europe for their poverty, corruption, porous borders, and lack of development. When the people of the EU were asked, in a 1999 survey, whether welcoming new countries should be a priority for the Union, six out of ten said no.

People in the acceding nations—which also include the island nations of Cyprus and Malta—have doubts of their own. Economically, they stand to gain from the influx of capital, jobs, and opportunity that Western Europe offers. But there will be growing pains too. Some will find their sense of nationhood subverted just a few short years after gaining independence; others will struggle as businesses born in the afterglow of socialism are forced to compete on a level playing field. As I traveled through the newcomer nations on the eve of the expansion, many people sounded like high school seniors on their way to the prom: excited, but riddled with insecurity and questions of identity. Do we measure up? Who will we become? Are we ready for this?

Good questions. These new members lag far behind the existing EU in many areas, from productivity and per capita income to life expectancy and health. Even those at the head of the class—Cyprus, Malta, Slovenia, and Estonia—will need several decades to catch up to the 15 older members. The others will take even longer.

Just getting to the starting line was a monumental task, since each nation was first required to overhaul its legal and financial systems to meet tough EU standards on trade, banking, business law, the environment, and minority rights. That transition has been far from painless: Ask the Hungarian winemaker whose wine, which once had home-field advantage due to import tariffs, must now compete with the best wines in Europe, or the retirees whose pensions, frozen in the name of fiscal austerity, haven't kept up with rising prices. "The rich get richer, the poor get poorer," said Helena Zapala, an earthy woman in her 60s who sells cheese on the streets of Kraków. "Where does that leave me?"

New members lag far behind the existing EU in many areas, from productivity and per capita income to life expectancy and health.

Also at risk are farmers, especially those in Poland, where they represent 20 percent of the population (versus 2 percent in the EU) but create less than 5 percent of the country's wealth. In a nation of more than 2 million farms, fewer than half are productive enough to qualify for EU support, which is given sparingly. The rest, now stripped of the Polish government subsidies that have kept them afloat since 1989, must fend for themselves.

"They're waiting for someone to tell them what to do," said Jacek Przybylski, a journalist for Polish TV who focuses on farming issues. "But from now on, no one will." Long revered as the backbone of the nation, farmers are feeling ill-equipped and helpless, trapped in the old mentality.

These were the issues debated during national referenda on EU accession. But in the end, voters in these countries, many caught for decades in the territorial brawl between the Soviet east and German west, may have simply embraced the first superpower that had the good manners to ask. "For Hungary, these two invitations—to join NATO in 1999 and the EU in May—were the first real signs that the Western world needs us," said Miklós Dérer, a national security expert in Budapest. "Our yes vote means we've made a choice to be Europeans, not Eastern Europeans. It means the end of ambiguity."

Home to 129,000 people and a half dozen large manufacturers, Győr, Hungary, illustrates the promise—and the pitfalls—of membership for the acceding countries. Győr owes its prosperity, and its low 4.5 percent unemployment rate, to EU-based companies like Volkswagen's Audi division, which moved here in 1993 to build engines, attracted by Hungary's low-cost workforce and its penchant for granting tax exemptions to foreign investors.

But Audi's tax breaks, it turns out, did not conform to EU law, and threatened to complicate Hungary's bid for membership. When the EU told Hungary such tax breaks would have to end, some worried about a mass exodus of manufacturers to less developed nations, where wages are dramatically lower. After two years of negotiations the EU agreed to grant Hungary a temporary exemption, and everyone breathed a sigh of relief. But the episode revealed a painful truth about life in the EU: The people of Győr—and Hungary—will be answering to Brussels from now on, and will be more vulnerable to forces beyond their direct control.

"There's a lot of fear in the air right now," said Steven Arnyek, a freelance photographer in Budapest. "What happens when one of these big foreign factories decides to pack up and leave? And how will our small businesses survive when they're totally unprepared to deal with EU regulations? These are just a few of the things our government has not yet bothered to explain. I'm for the EU—it's a necessity—but I also think it's going to be a catastrophe."

Despite the anxiety, there was no denying the palpable excitement I found among easterners who came of age after the fall of the Berlin Wall. "My daughter, who's 15, may grow up to feel more European than Czech. But most of all, she'll feel free. Hers is the first free generation," said Jiri Pehe, director of New York University in Prague, who fled communist Czechoslovakia in the trunk of a car in the 1980s and returned after the Wall came down. "Fifteen years ago my country was surrounded by watchtowers and barbed wire," he said. "Today we're surrounded by open borders."

In a Budapest café, an eager-faced woman in her 20s named Szilvia Pásztor said she's registered with an au pair agency so she can work in other EU countries—first in London ("to learn good English") and then in Paris. After Paris? "I not know," she said slowly, and beamed a broad smile glittering with new braces. "In the EU, everything possible!"

The tension between Europe's future and Europe's past is starkly evident in Estonia, one of three Baltic nations set to join the EU this month. Annexed by Stalin in 1940, overrun by the Nazis a year

---

Grow Today, Shrink Tomorrow?

The 10 new member nations have swollen the European Union's ranks to 455 million people. Despite that surge, the population tide will soon ebb. None of the 25 nations is producing enough babies to head off a downward trend. At current birthrates the EU's population will fall to 431 million by 2050. And as life expectancies rise, fewer workers will support more pensioners. "We need to bring our population back into balance," says EU Commissioner Anna Diamantopoulou. Yet resistance to a possible solution— increased immigration—remains high.

Will Economies Bloom or Bust?

The new EU countries face both economic opportunity and uncertainty as they plunge into a European single market. Some industries expect quick profits. In Hungary and the Czech Republic, the film and tourism sectors are poised for increased growth thanks to the nations' low costs, skilled labor, and rich scenery. Still, analysts predict it will take decades for most new members to reach the economic strength of older ones. Farmers are especially concerned: Most have small plots and outdated equipment but must compete with the EU's modern agribusinesses. Some observers worry that rough times could stoke nostalgia for communism. But at Budapest's Marxim café, communist icons serve capitalist purposes—they help sell pizza and beer. "This place represents something like a joke to young people," says 28-year-old Orsolya Galla. How do her parents feel? "They don't think much about communism anymore," she says. But her father, who relies on a state pension, remains unsure about the life in the EU. "He's worried," she says.

later, reconquered by the Soviets in 1944, liberated by the fall of communism in 1991, and invigorated by capitalism in the 1990s, Estonia is the whole drama in a nutshell.

I drove east on the highway that connects the capital of Tallinn with Narva, on the Russian border. Nearly everywhere I looked I saw the handiwork of the European Union, starting with the road itself. The EU has already invested millions of euros to improve the highway, which serves as the main link to St. Petersburg, Russia. This highway passes the town of Sillamäe, once a "closed" city run by the Soviet military, which enriched uranium for weapons programs in a huge factory overlooking the sea. The EU is here, too, kicking in more than a million dollars to help prevent the radioactive waste from leaching into the Baltic Sea. And at Narva, a city of 70,000, the EU is spending some 12 million dollars to upgrade the border crossing to deter illegal immigration, drugs, and human trade.

Capt. Jaanus Lumiste of the Border Guard had conducted three tours the week I arrived for various EU officials, who were suitably impressed with the state-of-the-art computer system, the 22 television monitors, the infrared scanner for bogus passports, and the no-nonsense approach of the Estonians manning the barricades. "Two million people crossed this border last year," Lumiste said with a slight smile, nodding at the bank of monitors. "Today we are ready."

Now that the border is fortified, Estonians are still pondering what to do with the 400,000 Russians in their midst, most descended from the thousands of Russians sent here, starting in the 1950s, to help control the openly defiant Estonians. This awkward relationship was turned upside down in 1991, when the Soviet army demobilized and the occupiers became uninvited houseguests. Many Russians assimilated, but 120,000 are Russian cit-

---

EU Enlarged

Perks and Burdens for the New Kids in the Bloc

Citizens of the 10 new EU members can count on major changes as their countries adjust to life in the 25-nation bloc. First, their businesses will gain easy access to a vast marketplace stretching from the Mediterranean to the Arctic. The result? "No longer will it take a mountain of paperwork and a whole day at customs to process goods coming in or going out of Slovenia," says Tomi Sefman, CEO of Slovenian bicycle maker Elan. As more goods circulate, consumers should get a wider selection and cheaper prices. Eventually workers will move as freely as the goods they produce, seeking jobs in any member country. But joining the EU has come at a cost. The new members each had to adopt 80,000 pages of new regulations and must now contribute to the Union's coffers. Initially most of the new members will receive more funds than they pay out: The EU has pledged to spend 28 billion dollars over the next three years to improve their infrastructure. Beyond economics, Lucia Antalova, a graduate student from Slovakia, sees a psychological benefit: "EU membership will draw a clean line between our future and our past."

---

izens who speak little or no Estonian yet have no intention of going home. Here again the EU has intervened, making fair treatment of the Russian minority a precondition for Estonia's membership.

Despite the shiny new EU presence in Estonia, there are still vestiges of the communist past. In Narva, just before dark, I came upon the last statue of Lenin still standing in Estonia. Cast in bronze and perhaps 20 feet tall, this figure once dominated the Narva town square, but in 1991, as Lenin statues all over Eastern Europe were being sledge-hammered into scrap metal, this one was moved to safety by local Russians. Today it's lodged in the side yard of a castle overlooking the Narva River. Though it was driving rain, I got out of my car for a closer look, which is when I noticed the flowers. Strewn across the base of the statue, between Lenin's boots, were dozens of carnations and roses, placed there, I supposed, by local Russians. Like flowers on a grave, they were wilted and sad in the gathering gloom, dead but not yet buried.

Failures of history are of little interest to Stanislaw Nowak, the Polish fruit grower, who spends his time thinking about the future. But Nowak is no idle dreamer: Over the past few years he and wife Anna have turned their rustic farm in Małopolska into a model of EU compliance. They were, in fact, the first farmers in their district to apply for an EU subsidy, which provides matching funds to help farmers update their operations. Unlike most of their neighbors, the Nowaks had the capital, the acreage, the persistence, and the business plan to back up their application, which was approved by Brussels in 2003.

As Nowak showed me his orchards in the waning light of a winter day, his enthusiasm for his family's future, and Poland's, rose as the temperature dropped. He is optimistic, he says, not because he has forgotten the past, but because he remembers it clearly. "We lived through the Nazis and we lived through the Communists," he said with a dismissive laugh. "So we are not afraid of the European Union."

EU Expansion Brings Expectations, Fears for New Members

By Roger Wilkison
Voice of America News, May 1, 2004

Ten new members—mostly former communist countries—are joining the European Union on Saturday in the bloc's biggest-ever expansion. For the newcomers, EU membership is the best available guarantee of peace, freedom, and future prosperity. But they are also aware that they have to work hard to catch up with the wealthier countries to the west.

Lithuania, like its Baltic neighbors Estonia and Latvia, was occupied by the former Soviet Union for 50 years and thus cut off from the rest of Europe.

It has labored hard to overcome the legacy of those years, represented by a crumbling infrastructure, environmental pollution, and the corruption associated with the old Soviet-style bureaucracy.

With one of the lowest per capita incomes of the new EU members, it raced to catch up and, last year, its economy grew by nearly 9 percent, largely due to massive foreign investment spurred by a low corporate tax rate.

Overseeing that process was Finance Minister Dalia Grybauskaite, who also imposed tight controls on government spending and sold off inefficient state-owned companies. She says her fellow-citizens think Lithuania's entry into the EU will boost living standards and open up new markets for Lithuanian products.

"For ordinary Lithuanians, the hopes are, of course, historically based on looking for political security, economic security, and a more prosperous life," she said. "I think, in the near future, we don't fear too much and, for ordinary people, they do not yet know what to fear. And I'm happy about that because I think we feared so much in our history and we have gone through such difficult times that we don't think that the European Union will be something to fear seriously about."

Ms. Grybauskaite says the only thing that seems to bother Lithuanians is EU bureaucracy, with its requirements that the new member states measure up to often rigid standards in such areas as food safety and pollution controls.

Article in the public domain.

That is a criticism that is common elsewhere in the Baltic States. Latvian president Vaira Vike-Freiberga recently told reporters in Brussels that EU regulations are cumbersome but are outweighed by her country's access to a single market of 455 million consumers.

"Certainly, we are gaining this very large market which actually will now be larger than the United States in terms of numbers of inhabitants," said Ms. Vike-Freiberga. "The losses are that this market, in order to have access to it, we have to comply with this enormous body of severe restrictions and severe requirements."

Polls show that most citizens of the Baltic states believe EU membership will bring them better living standards. But Audrius Matonis, the chief editor of the Baltic News Service in Lithuania, says there is also widespread concern that prices will rise.

"The main fear is that some prices, for food, let's say, for petroleum, for cigarettes, will rise," he said. "So that's why some groups of people are buying even now sugar, salt, some other products, because of the fears that the prices are going up."

And those fears are not limited to the Baltic countries. Lena Kolarska Bobinska, who heads the Committee on Public Affairs, a research organization in Warsaw, says Poland, too, has been hit by fears of price rises.

Polls show that most citizens of the Baltic states believe EU membership will bring them better living standards.

"Suddenly there is gossip that the price of sugar will go up," she said. "So, like in the period of communism, everybody is running to the shop and buying sugar and hiding it because the price will be bigger. Even some marketing companies are building their market campaigns on that fear, saying 'were you told that the prices will go down?' And there is a big question mark suggesting that prices will not go down, that you were cheated, that prices will go up."

But Ms. Bobinska says those fears have still not dissuaded Poles from believing that they must continue on the road of EU membership, even if they realize it will not always be a joyful ride.

Experts say any price increases will be minor, and will likely be followed by wage increases in the years to come.

Pawel Swieboda, the head of the Polish foreign ministry's European Integration department, says change always provokes fear and unease.

"The fears concern mainly the competitive pressures, which will come as we join the European Union," said Pawel Swieboda. "Obviously, the economies of the current member states are much more advanced than our own. Our own is really dynamic. We're growing at five percent, but, still, there is a catch-up process to go through. And the sooner we do it, the better."

But Mr. Swieboda argues that any momentary dislocations are far outweighed by what EU membership will bring Poland after decades of war, communist domination, and the painful adjustment to a market economy.

"There is certainly a great expectation that by returning to Europe—because that's the way we prefer to see it—we will enhance our own stability, we will enhance our economic growth," he said. "And there is something more spiritual, I suppose, that it will enhance our sense of belonging and that identity-wise, we'll find ourselves in a much different situation, in a situation of certainty."

So, Europe has finally bridged the divide caused by the 20th century's hot and cold wars, and most of its countries are united in what the EU likes to call "a community of shared values." Now the hard part begins, making sure that EU membership delivers prosperity to what are still relatively poor countries, and narrows the gap between them and their richer western partners.

European Integration Unplugged

BY MARTIN RÜCKER
FOREIGN POLICY, SEPTEMBER 2004

Halfway between Lithuania's capital of Vilnius and its second-largest city, Kaunas, on the surprisingly smooth two-lane highway that bisects the country from east to west, three red-and-white striped smokestacks poke into the sky. Only one is smoking, sending forth a thin, solitary plume that trails over the forests and meadows of the small town of Elektrenai, population 14,000. During the 1960s, the town's power plant—a model of centrally planned gigantism—helped spark an industrial boom across Soviet-era Lithuania and the surrounding Baltic States. But with the construction of a huge nuclear power plant in the 1970s and 1980s in Ignalina to the northeast, Elektrenai's turbines largely fell silent, its familiar smokestacks becoming little more than a landmark for passing truckers and motorists.

Now, in one of those twists of geopolitical fate, Lithuania's entry into the European Union (EU) last May holds out the promise of Elektrenai's salvation. The EU has declared Ignalina's Chernobyl-style reactors a dangerous powder keg and insisted that Lithuania remove them from the electricity grid, or forgo EU membership. Policymakers in Vilnius grudgingly agreed, in return for an initial payment from Brussels of 285 million euros over the next two years to decommission Ignalina and transform Elektrenai once again into the Baltics' largest energy producer.

With this one stroke, the EU is writing one of the more bizarre chapters in the story of its eastward expansion. In a previous era, the Kremlin's grand industrial dreams drove rapid change in Lithuania and other countries in Eastern Europe. Today, change is driven by the EU's belief that growth cannot come at the expense of public health, safety, or the environment. As benevolent as that diktat may seem, once again a distant capital—this time Brussels, not Moscow—is handing down a blueprint for economic transformation. And, once again, the inhabitants of a small community, still reeling from their last exercise in social and economic engineering, must play catch-up by someone else's rules. Never mind the underlying irony that Elektrenai's Communist dynamos have become the engine for the country's capitalist transformation.

Lithuania: From Soviet Union to European Union

Location: Borders the Baltic Sea, between Russia, Poland, Belarus, and Latvia

Population: 3.6 million

Government Type: Parliamentary democracy

Gross Domestic Product per capita: $11,200

Unemployment Rate: 10.7 percent

Forcibly annexed by the USSR in 1940, Lithuania became the first Soviet republic to declare its independence on March 11, 1990. Thirteen years later, more than 63 percent of Lithuanians turned out for a referendum on European Union (EU) accession, with 91 percent voting in favor of joining the EU.

Beginning in 1992, with the assistance of the International Monetary Fund, Lithuania implemented a series of economic reforms, including privatization, tax reform, and reduced government spending. In recent years, the country has shown rapid economic growth (7.7 percent alone in the first quarter of 2004), earning it the moniker "the Baltic Tiger." Yet Lithuania's gross domestic product (GDP) per capita is still 46 percent of the EU average, as compared to 113 percent for France and 107 percent for Italy. In terms of GDP per capita, Lithuania ranks 23rd among the 25 current EU members (tied with Poland, and ranked above only Latvia).

Relations between Lithuania and Russia remain frosty, due in part to Moscow's concerns about the rights and status of ethnic Russians and Russian-speaking Lithuanians, who compose 9.1 percent of Lithuania's population.

Europe's wider, increasingly ambitious union depends on the ability of Elektrenai and hundreds of towns like it to make EU expansion a success.

Power and the Powerless

"Communism," Vladimir Lenin said, "is Soviet power plus the electrification of the whole country." Elektrenai was built as a model of both. Like the Czech Republic's planned community of Kuncice or Poland's iconic metallurgical-works town of Nowa Huta, Elektrenai was conceived from scratch as an international advertisement for socialism, with broad, straight avenues, prefabricated housing blocks, and—a first for the predominantly Catholic Lithuania—no church. Visitors from across the Soviet Union came for guided tours of this masterpiece of Communist planning.

One man who was present at the creation is Pranas Noreika, the director of Elektrenai's power station since its birth in 1960. A tall man, hard of hearing, wearing thick glasses and white tennis socks under wool pants, Noreika holds forth from his office, complete with black leather sofa, red conference table, handsome wooden desk, and wine cabinet. A good engineer who professes indifference to party politics, Noreika knows the right people. Almost every Sunday he entertains Prime Minister Algirdas Brazauskas, a friend since their days together at university. The two white-haired survivors trade their business suits for swim trunks and enter the sauna at the power station, putting the world to rights.

A member of the Communist Party, Noreika nonetheless implemented his own brand of socialism. He ensured that hundreds of Lithuanians once banished to Siberia under Soviet premier Joseph Stalin later found jobs and homes in Elektrenai. Behind Moscow's back, some locals say, he turned planned warehouses into sport facilities, including the country's premier hockey stadium, where U.S. National Hockey League stars Darius Kasparaitis and Dainius Zubrus learned to skate. One business trip to Moscow yielded a Gorki Park roller coaster destined for the scrapheap, "Jet Star 2"; a Ferris wheel followed, and soon, tiny Elektrenai claimed the largest amusement park in the Baltics. Right up until Moscow recognized Lithuania's independence in 1991, Noreika was busy drawing up plans for a new downtown area and a cultural complex where music and art groups would practice and perform. "If perestroika hadn't come about," he says, "we'd have built it all."

After independence in 1991, an elected council gradually took over most of the town's property. Elektrenai's first and only church opened, built badly but big, in the socialist style. Soon afterward, a storm toppled two of its concrete towers. The rest of the town fared little better. In Soviet times, thousands of tourists from all over the country visited the amusement park every weekend. Today, the colorful lights are dark, the music has gone silent, and the roller coaster rusts away. Most of the time, the park's employees sit idly on a bench in front of the ticket window. "People don't have the money to come here," one of them says. The swimming baths have closed. The diving tower at the lake is dilapidated, the yacht club vacant. There are too many buildings to maintain in this tiny town, now that it has to survive on its own.

Surrounded by anachronism, the people of Elektrenai cannot help but be pessimistic. Vendors in the local markets wax nostalgic about business during the Soviet era, and their customers complain of high unemployment and poverty. Yet Elektrenai is relatively well off. At 5.3 percent, unemployment is lower here than in all of Lithuania, with a national average of 10.7 percent. Nobody in the town seems aware of that fact. Even as Lithuania's politicians look to the EU as a way of breaking with the Soviet past, young people dream of "moving west" instead of bringing "the West" to their own country. They see workers in Old Europe earning many times their salaries. For the young, the only way to build a future seems to be to abandon their past.

Such a luxury is not available to the 76-year-old Noreika, charged with making his old power station fit for a new Europe. Already, the former Soviet official has transformed the plant into a joint-stock company. Soon, its four 300-megawatt units and four 150-megawatt units will get a high-tech overhaul. Noreika's crews have to install new burners and gas-cleaning equipment. They must replace the plant's control devices and instruments, refurbish its steam turbines, and automate much of the generator and turbine maintenance. New sulfur filters will improve the town's air quality: If the plant operated at full capacity today, people say, the birds of Elektrenai would fall out of the sky.

But introducing free-market efficiencies may be Noreika's biggest challenge. The plant remains grossly overstaffed, a typical problem at large state enterprises everywhere. Many of the laborers who retire are not replaced. For the rest of the workforce, Noreika tries to invent new tasks. But workers still struggle to fill their days—with, rumor has it, card games and long breaks. One worker tells of how "repairs" are still carried out in the old way: with a fresh coat of paint and polish. Even as Lithuania's leaders celebrate their new European identity, the "old way" remains everywhere in Elektrenai: in habit, nostalgia, and fear of what is to come.

Plugging In

More than 90 percent of Lithuanian voters chose to join the EU in last year's referendum.

Noreika championed membership in the EU and tried to recruit his workers to that cause. Ultimately, more than 90 percent of Lithuanian voters chose to join the EU in last year's referendum. Many of Elektrenai's workers have long dreamed that the EU would bring an economic upturn and new jobs. But according to Jurgis Vilemas, director of the Lithuanian Energy Institute, only 600 of the 800 jobs will remain after renovations at the plant are completed. With privatization, 200 or 300 more jobs will have to go.

Kestutis Vaitukaitis, mayor of the Elektrenai district, plans to woo EU investors. He believes Elektrenai could become a sort of Lithuanian Disneyland—"Energoland," he calls it. With a new roller coaster, a renovated yacht club, and a new ice stadium, he hopes tourists will come in droves. Soon, he predicts, they will bathe in the lake before a backdrop of three smoking chimneys. But this feels like a fantasy, an echo of Soviet ways: trying to do everything as big and as fast as possible, whether a market exists or not. In reality, Vaitukaitis is having a hard time luring any business, let alone tourists, to this remote industrial town. One young woman, a 25-year-old teacher named Justina, points out the Russian music still playing at Elektrenai's lakeside cafe. It's like a time warp, as if the winds of political change had passed Elektrenai by. "Why doesn't the mayor do something?" Justina asks. Just as in the Soviet era, the people are waiting for a plan.

Capitalism requires more patience. The great European unification, after all, will come about by installment. There are still passport controls at the borders, and it will take years before the citizens of Elektrenai are spending euros at the local grocery store. A free labor market is a long way off. Noreika seems to grasp this—which is fortunate, because neither the Eurocrats in Brussels nor the mayor can match his influence in the town he has run for most of the last half century. I ask him how long he plans to keep working. "Till all three chimneys are smoking again," he answers, with a smile. It seems not even he knows whether he is kidding.

Second-class Allies

By John Kampfner
New Statesman, April 19, 2004

I don't imagine there are that many Slovaks who have seen a bloke in a skirt. As James McCarthy, a burly Scotsman, walked through the cobbled streets of Bratislava's old town, he was the object of much giggling and finger-pointing. A piper from the Black Watch regiment, he was an unlikely emissary for Britain on a day rich in symbolism. This was 2 April, and a few hours earlier Slovakia and six other former communist states had, at a ceremony in Brussels, joined NATO. On 1 May a similar group of nations will accede to the European Union. The dismemberment of the Soviet empire, first dreamt of by Ronald Reagan and Margaret Thatcher, will be complete.

McCarthy put it in less grandiose terms. "It's a great day for these people," he said. "I feel so happy for them." Our conversation was interrupted as locals, among them uniformed Slovak squaddies and their girlfriends, lined up to be photographed next to him. Then he entertained them with a turn on his bagpipes before an American military band playing Joe Cocker and cover versions of pop tunes by other artists took over. Hviezdoslavovo Námestie, one of Bratislava's main squares, where in years gone by torchlit marches proclaimed the virtues of the socialist brotherhood, teemed with NATO flags.

So much for predictions at the end of the cold war that the Atlantic Alliance would wither away. It is a remarkable transformation, one that could have begun only in that brief window of opportunity in the mid- to late 1990s, when Boris Yeltsin was in no state to object. "We would never have got it through in the present circumstances," said a senior UK diplomat, referring to the chill in relations between the West and the Russia of President Vladimir Putin.

The celebrations were replicated in other countries. They mark the biggest and strategically most important expansion in NATO's 55-year history. But they were deliberately low-key, in recognition not just of Russian sensibilities but of the mixed feelings voters in the new member countries have towards the organisations to which they are linking their future. Hostility is even more marked in attitudes towards the EU than towards NATO. The eight formerly communist accession states—Poland, Hungary, the Czech Republic, Slovakia, Slovenia, and the Baltic states of Latvia, Lithuania, and

Estonia—have been required to open up their markets and reform their economies in just a few years. They have done so with varying degrees of enthusiasm and success.

In Slovakia, one of the poorest, steep tax increases on goods and services took effect in January, and more changes are scheduled for May. VAT [value-added tax on purchases] rose to 19 per cent for basics such as bread,

> *Leaders are counting on enlargement to provide jobs, foreign investment, tourism, and exports.*

water, and medicine. At the same time, social benefit cheques were trimmed and government institutions including the armed forces and the state-run railways started cutting jobs. Thousands of small businesses that could not comply with EU-related rules have closed. Slovakia's unemployment rate has reached 16 per cent. Budget reforms and job cuts have led to strikes and protests involving everyone from students and civil servants to doctors and pharmacists. Hardest hit has been the impoverished Roma [gypsy] minority mainly in eastern Slovakia. In February, thousands of troops and police were deployed to stop looting from food shops.

Throughout the unrest Slovakia's centre-right prime minister, Mikuláš Dzurinda, and his counterpart in the wealthier Czech Republic, Vladimír Špidla, have vowed to stay the course. Within three months of Dzurinda's re-election in 2002 he was rewarded with offers of membership of both NATO and the EU. Since the reforms began to bite, however, his grip on power has loosened.

Both leaders are counting on enlargement to provide jobs, foreign investment, tourism, and exports. Their first major success has come in the motor industry, with Toyota building a factory in the Czech Republic and Hyundai picking Slovakia for a similar plant that will be worth 1.1bn euros and will produce 300,000 cars a year. With Peugeot Citroën and Volkswagen already there, Slovakia will produce more cars per head of population than any other country in the world. The Koreans said they chose it over Poland partly because of better road and rail links to the rest of Europe, and partly because of a staggeringly low flat rate of corporate and income tax: 19 per cent.

The bottom line for all these countries, however, was reciprocal access to the rest of the EU for the Union's 73 million new citizens. They did not expect that all 15 existing members would impose restrictions (although Britain's hasty response has been to restrict welfare rights but not work).

The sense of discrimination and humiliation is strong. A poll conducted recently for the government in Poland, where unemployment is running at more than 20 per cent, found that just 10 per cent of voters believed EU membership would produce a better standard of living. The reaction in Hungary has been similarly hostile, but for different reasons. Hungary's economy is considerably healthier than those of some of the established states. Its jobless rate of 5.9 per cent compares favourably to the 11 per cent in Spain, 10 per cent in France and 9 per cent in Germany. It is thinking of imposing its own restrictions, partly for revenge and partly because, it says, it wants from abroad only people with skills or serious money to invest.

Many voters fear that rich foreigners will not only push up property prices, but that they will buy up swathes of farmland and other assets.

The mood has swung in only 12 months since the referendums in which voters overwhelmingly backed EU membership (albeit with low turnouts in some countries). I met a group of students who voiced the deep-seated scepticism one now finds in the region. "It's fine for people like you to come for the weekend for our cheap beer," said Martina, noting with disdain the various British stag parties that descend on the capital, "but what do we get in return?" With no memory of dictatorship, her generation takes free speech and free travel for granted.

Two days after the NATO celebrations in Bratislava, Slovaks voted for Vladimír Meciar in the first round of their presidential election. Meciar, a former boxer and prime minister between 1994 and 1998, is seen by Western governments as corrupt and hostile to both the Atlantic Alliance and the EU. His comeback highlights the disquiet Slovaks feel about their new allies. A similar backlash may take place elsewhere.

Anxieties over the economy and national identity have been compounded by another fear—vulnerability to terrorism. Most of these "emerging" countries supported the Bush administration in its war on Iraq. Now they fear they may pay the price. Countries such as Romania and Bulgaria were quick to open their bases and airspace to U.S. troops on their way to Afghanistan in 2001. They soon contributed troops of their own. Both are now likely to play host to permanent U.S. bases. Polish and Slovak forces are involved in Iraq. As for the Hungarians, they did not appreciate being lied to by the Americans on the eve of war. The U.S. said it needed a large airbase in the country to "train translators." It later emerged that the base had been temporary home to an Iraqi administration-in-waiting.

With little thanks from the U.S. for their armed forces being targeted in Iraq—and with little reward from "old Europe," led by France and Germany, for joining the EU—many in these countries wonder whether they have made the right choices. In reality, they had little alternative. In any case, the die is cast.

Turks Worry That a Union With Europe Will Cost Them Their Soul

By Susan Sachs
The New York Times, December 17, 2004

As a businessman, Zeki Baykam can list the economic benefits of Turkey's joining the European Union one day. Foreign investment is one. Manageable inflation is another. In terms of his concrete company, he said, "we might finally be able to plan the future."

But like many people who are waiting nervously to see if Europe wants Turkey, Mr. Baykam is less concerned about the destination than the journey.

"What we're interested in is the rules part," he said, referring to the standards that his country would be expected to adopt on the road to membership in the 25-nation bloc. "Human rights, justice, the rule of law—those are our aims. Those values are more important than the economy."

Europe has long been Turkey's obsession, firing the desires of the Ottoman sultans and portrayed as the model of civilization. Joining the European Union has preoccupied Turkish governments on and off for more than 40 years.

[In Brussels on Thursday, diplomats said that the bloc's 25 presidents and prime ministers would announce Friday that Turkey would be invited to accession talks next October, though the conditions remained to be negotiated. The talks, they cautioned, could last for years.]

The prospect of Muslim Turkey's membership has set off a storm of public opposition in Europe. It has also set Turks on a soul-searching analysis of where they belong and what they want. As the price of joining the European club, they have found themselves under Europe's microscope—scrutinized, evaluated, chided, and instructed—and the experience has proved unsettling.

In interviews in Turkey's Anatolian heartland, a region of citrus groves in the south and snow-dusted highlands in the north, most people spoke of the accession process as their best hope for guaranteeing individual freedoms and forcing financial discipline on the government.

But, in a common subtheme, they also expressed resentment that some Europeans questioned their credentials and their treatment of religious and ethnic minorities. Proud of their Ottoman Empire heritage, they bristled at being in the position of supplicants to the politicians of Europe.

At the same time, most people expressed admiration for Prime Minister Recep Tayyip Erdogan's full-throttle push for European acceptance. But they also worried that Mr. Erdogan, who entered politics by way of an Islamic fundamentalist party, might abandon his Western-oriented policies or lose power if the European Union piles on too many conditions.

"Right now everybody is for him and his party, but that's tied to this EU process," said Burhan Cagdas, a restaurant owner near the ancient bazaar of Gaziantep, a sprawling city four hours east of the citrus groves of Adana. "But I'd say everyone is waiting. It's possible that if there is a negative outcome, he could revert to his Islamist roots. But I think he has changed and grown wiser."

Two flights up a steep stone staircase from his busy kebab restaurant, in a white-tiled room foggy with flour, Mr. Cagdas presided over a crew of men in surgical masks who rhythmically pressed out sheet after papery sheet of dough with their yardlong wooden rolling pins.

They were making baklava, the pistachio pastry drowned in liquefied sugar that is a specialty of Gaziantep. Except for the presence of a machine that rolls out the first nickel-thick slab of dough, Mr. Cagdas said nothing about the process has changed since his family started the baklava business in 1887.

To him, joining the European Union would be an affirmation of another Turkish tradition that has been stifled in recent decades. "We had the tradition of diversity, of living side by side with different kinds of people," he said. "I think it's better that way. It's richer and more colorful."

East of Gaziantep, past the fertile banks of the Euphrates River, the landscape and the outlook become bleaker. Around the town of Sanliurfa, near ancient ruins where the biblical prophet Abraham is reputed to have lived, tribal loyalties and religious conservatism maintain a hold on the people.

So do powerful men like Nahit Koran, a hereditary landlord with control over thousands of acres, several hardscrabble villages, and the fortunes of his tenants.

Mr. Koran owns the houses where they live and he pays them a fixed wage for their labor on his land. He said he also mediated their disputes, paid the bride price when the young men wanted to marry, and sent them to the hospital when they were sick.

Driving to one of his remote villages, a dot of small dwellings on the carpet of rocky earth and tilled fields, he watched as men, women and children bent nearly double to harvest knee-high cotton plants.

"What I don't like is that those European countries with a bar-baric background are now trying to teach us how to live," Mr. Koran said. "Snobbish people come from Europe and say, 'You can't have women working and kids working.' They forget about the days when 12-year-olds worked in the coal mines of England."

Mr. Koran is a member of the Nationalist Movement party, a small but vocal ultranationalist group that views European Union membership as a trap for Turkey and a threat to its sovereignty. Western powers tried to carve up the exhausted Ottoman Empire nearly a century ago, said Mr. Koran, and the European Union will try to do the same.

"Soon we will see their real faces," he added. "That's why it's non-sense for Turkey to join the EU."

While Mr. Koran's views represent the more extreme range of Turkish public opinion, even moderate Turks have bridled at the constant flow of outside criticism and analysis that has come with their application to join the European Union.

"I don't consider Europe, or for that matter, the United States, as a prototype," said Mustafa Coskun, the head of the local bar associ-

---

"What I don't like is that those European countries with a barbaric background are now trying to teach us how to live."—Nahit
Koran, a hereditary landlord

---

ation in Sivas, a tough working-class city in the highlands of Ana-tolia.

Turkey should not be treated as a backward country in need of fixing, but as a major European power like France or Germany, he added. "Otherwise, what's the point of joining the EU?"

Earlier this month, the president of the European Parliament set the country on edge by referring to the largely Kurdish-populated southeast region as "Kurdistan," prompting media speculation that Europe's hidden agenda was to split the country along ethnic or religious lines.

The issue is particularly delicate in Sivas, which has been trying to live down an image of religious intolerance formed in 1993. Then, 37 people died after Muslim fundamentalists set fire to a hotel where a conference with secular intellectuals and Turkish Alawites, a minority Muslim sect, was being held.

Tens of thousands of Alawites, whose ancestors had lived for cen-turies in the plains near Sivas, fled to Istanbul. Those who remained see Europe as a possible protector of religious freedom. But they are also uneasy with being singled out as a minority.

"We don't consider ourselves a minority," said Ertugrul Arslan, an Alawite community leader in Sivas. "We are part of this society. Defining us as a minority is a provocation."

At the same time, Mr. Arslan added, "we don't want to say or do anything that would be an obstacle to Turkey's path to the EU."

III. Trade and Finance

Editor's Introduction

The European Union's economy is a powerhouse at present but has a less certain prospect for the future. Today it is one of the strongest economies in the world, outdoing the United States in most respects and showing a trade surplus rather than a deficit. However, the European Union does not surpass the United States in productivity, which means that it may be overtaken in the future by the United States or by one of Asia's burgeoning superpowers (China or India). Economists also worry that an aging population will make the EU less and less competitive and undermine its ability to offer the range of social services most of its citizens expect; some even fear outbreaks of civil disorder. A more immediate concern is the weakening dollar, which threatens to curtail Europe's lucrative export trade with the United States.

This uncertain future is in contrast to the cheery present, however. One of the EU's most dramatic successes was the introduction, in 2002, of a single European currency. The euro (€) was adopted by 12 of the 15 member nations of the day, with only Denmark, Great Britain, and Sweden retaining their own national currencies. A hypothetical euro had been the basis for rates of exchange among the various European countries since 1999, but in 2002 real euros entered people's daily lives.* In "Few Problems in Euro Takeover," David Rising of the Associated Press describes the surprisingly smooth transition as the new coins and bills went into circulation, replacing a dozen old currencies. Many of the new member states that entered the Union in 2004 would like to adopt the euro too, but so far none of them can meet the strict requirements of the Maastricht Treaty, as Mark Landler explains in a *New York Times* article, "Europe's New Members Not Ready for the Euro." The fact that some of the established members are also in violation of Maastricht's requirements, with deficits above 3 percent of gross domestic product, is annoying to East European leaders but hardly the worst problem they face. Indeed, EU aid is essential to the new member states, if they are ever going to catch up with the more prosperous nations of the West.

The struggling economies of the new member states tend to slow the progress of the EU as a whole, reports the *EUobserver*'s Richard Carter in "Europe's Society Under Strain, Says Leaked Economic Report." The report in question, assessing the EU's progress toward creating the world's most competitive economy by 2010, described the Union as less than halfway to its goal and in danger of a precipitous economic decline unless it can adhere to the "Lisbon Agenda," as its master plan is called. Although the EU has created over 6 million new jobs in the past five years, it will need almost twice as many to achieve a 70 percent employment rate by 2010, and the looming dilemmas posed by an aging population have yet to be addressed.

In "Beyond Integration," from the journal *Finance & Development*, Michael Deppler analyzes the European approach to economic policy, an approach that involves the careful balancing of social benefits with fiscal stability, sometimes to the detriment of growth. Europe's lagging productivity is a persistent problem but not beyond solution, Deppler believes, if only the electorate can be persuaded to accept long-term reforms.

The areas most resistant to reform include agriculture, which is heavily subsidized in many European countries (as it is also, in different ways, in the United States and Canada). In May 2004 the EU offered to drop its export subsidies for agricultural products if other developed nations would make parallel concessions. As Constant Brand reports for the Associated Press in "EU Offers to Eliminate Its Farm Export Subsidies at World Trade Talks," the EU was responding to complaints by underdeveloped nations that its agricultural policies made competition impossible and stifled development in the Third World.

Finally, in "Old Continent, New Deal," published in the American Bar Association's *ABA Journal*, Martha Neil lays out the legal complexities of doing business in Europe, where lawyers for American firms must be familiar with overarching EU regulations as well as the national laws of 25 different countries. Although the development of the EU has led to welcome standardization in some areas, such as trademark protection and financial reporting, it has also given strength and scope to European concerns about fair competition, fair labor practices, and environmental impact, which are defined differently overseas. The European market is extremely important to American manufacturers and businessmen, however, and the EU is a much safer place to open a branch office than, say, South America or Central Asia, so American lawyers are now busily studying EU regulations and seeking contacts abroad to negotiate new deals.

Few Problems in Euro Takeover

By David Rising
Associated Press, January 2, 2002

Cashiers across Europe were on the front lines of the largest currency changeover in history Wednesday, taking on the central role of getting old money out of circulation and new euros into the pockets of consumers.

At the Kaufland supermarket chain in Berlin, cashier Isabell Schosstag greeted every customer with the same question: "Will you be paying in euros or Deutsche marks?"

The question was echoed in other languages, about other currencies, across the 12-nation euro zone on the first full day of business since the bills and coins were introduced Jan. 1.

Minor glitches aside, concerns that the transition would evoke "euro-rage" from frustrated consumers appeared unfounded.

Schosstag said weeks of reading about the euro and its security features—and even several days of "euro-school"—gave her confidence. Yet she took special care when counting the change back to customers, laying each coin out deliberately.

"It's a little slower because you have to concentrate more, and you also have to make double sure of the change you're giving, but nobody's asking any questions," Schosstag said.

About a third of Schosstag's customers paid in the new currency, a third in the Deutsche mark, and a third with their debit cards. The store had boosted the number of cashiers by a third to prevent long lines.

"I brought a bunch of my old change and had no problems," said Karin Krebs, who paid for groceries with a handful of mark coins she wanted to get rid of. "I have euros at home, though."

Krebs' experience is just what European Central Bank officials have been hoping for. The bank intends to vacuum most of the old currencies from circulation within two weeks by asking retailers to give euros as change and by having ATMs dispense only the new bills.

Still, in many places, to spare confusion, clerks were giving change in the outgoing currencies if customers paid in them.

After the first day of the changeover, 80 percent of the euro zone's 200,000 ATMs were dispensing euros, with the figure reaching 100 percent in Austria, Germany, Luxembourg, and the Netherlands. Demand for money from the machines reached four times the daily average on Jan. 1, the European Central Bank said.

"The euro cash changeover is going smoothly, even better than we had expected," the bank's Eugenio Domingo Solans said.

As of midday, the euro had surged in value from 88 U.S. cents to more than 90 U.S. cents, largely because the successful changeover has created a sense of confidence, said market analyst Dorothea Huttanus, of DZ Bank.

There were, however, some hitches reported in almost all countries.

Traffic backed up on toll booths outside Athens, Greece, on highways in Italy, and on the main bridge into Lisbon, Portugal, as drivers tried to get euros as change from attendants. Authorities appealed to drivers to use exact change.

> *"The euro cash changeover is going smoothly, even better than we had expected."*—
> **Eugenio Domingo Solans, European Central Bank**

Lines were longer than usual at some banks and post offices. In Naples, Italy, police were called when retirees waiting for their first euro pensions got unruly. To help foster acceptance of the new currency, Greek premier Costas Simitis visited five banks in Athens and asked customers to show patience.

Bank unions in France and Italy tried to stage strikes but drew little support and caused only minor disruptions.

In Ireland, many complained that some pubs were already rejecting old Irish coins because two sets of change was proving too burdensome.

Officials warned shoppers to beware of salespeople giving incorrect change. But the difficulty of the new conversions was evident when reporters asked Portuguese finance minister Guilherme Oliveira Martins to give the escudo equivalent of 100 euros.

"That's . . . er . . . well, it's going to take some time to get used to it all," he replied.

Some stores even used the confusion as a marketing tool.

The big German supermarket chain Aldi rounded prices down, resulting in price cuts averaging 2 to 3 percent. Rival Rewe dropped prices on about 250 items and promised it wouldn't raise any prices, and Kaufland boasted that prices on 1,300 items were lower than before.

The euro was actually introduced in 1999, when national currencies were pegged to it at fixed rates and ceased to trade independently, but the paper money first became available on Jan. 1. National currencies will continue to circulate side by side with the euro for up to two months.

Austria, Belgium, Finland, France, Germany, Greece, Ireland, Italy, Luxembourg, the Netherlands, Portugal, and Spain make up the new euro-zone. The European Union countries of Britain, Sweden, and Denmark have opted out.

Europe's New Members Not Ready for the Euro

BY MARK LANDLER
THE NEW YORK TIMES, OCTOBER 21, 2004

Six months after the European Union admitted 10 new members, capping their journey from communism to the free market, they got a blunt reminder that the club's inner sanctum, its currency union, will remain off limits to them for several years.

The European Central Bank said in a report issued Wednesday that fewer than half the new members had met the fiscal requirements to adopt the euro. None had met the political requirements, like compatibility of its central bank statutes with those of the European Central Bank, according to a companion report by the European Commission.

The bank, the currency's guardian, said many of the countries were moving too slowly in cutting their budget deficits to levels below the ceiling mandated by the Maastricht Treaty, which created the monetary union.

"They have their weak points and they have their strong points, and life is difficult for all of them," said the president of the bank, Jean-Claude Trichet, at a news conference here [in Frankfurt, Germany].

Mr. Trichet said there was no timetable for countries to adopt the euro, echoing what is by now the conventional wisdom here: with the exception of Estonia and one or two of its Baltic neighbors, none of these countries will be ready for the euro until the end of the decade.

That is a remarkable turnabout from the heady days just before the expansion of the European Union, when political leaders in Budapest, Prague, Warsaw, and Bratislava talked about adopting the euro in short order. Now, in Prague, the finance ministry and the central bank are squabbling about whether the Czech Republic can meet even the less ambitious deadline of 2010.

The reason for much of the backsliding, experts say, is the political upheaval that erupted in many countries after they entered the Union. The collapse of coalition governments and a revolving door of prime ministers has scrambled fiscal policies and raised doubts about the independence of their central banks.

"Some countries that were ahead fell back, in the context of elections," said Otmar Issing, the bank's chief economist, who oversaw the report. "That is the normal process in a democracy."

Critics say that Europe's demand for fiscal discipline is ringing hollow.

In some countries, the political tumult is taking on a less-than-democratic flavor. Hungary's newly elected prime minister, Ferenc Gyurcsány, is pushing legislation in Parliament that would allow him to appoint half the members of the governing board of the central bank.

Mr. Gyurcsány, a millionaire businessman and one-time communist youth leader, is unhappy that the central bank has set interest rates at 11 percent—the highest in Europe—to curb Hungary's high 6.6 percent inflation. The new law, if approved, could tilt the board in favor of the prime minister.

"It's very dangerous," said a former president of the Hungarian central bank, Péter Ákos Bod, in an interview. "It goes very much against European custom, and against the short history of the bank."

Hungary's high rates are necessary to prevent runaway inflation, Mr. Bod said. The answer to the government's woes, he said, is to curb state borrowing. Its budget deficit is equal to 5.5 percent of gross domestic product—well above the 3 percent cap mandated by Brussels.

The Czech Republic has also struggled to stem a tide of red ink. Its deficit peaked at 12.6 percent of gross domestic product in 2003, before falling to an estimated 5 percent this year. That volatility prompted the deputy governor of the Czech central bank, Ludek Niedermayer, to question whether the country will achieve its goal of reducing the deficit to below 3 percent by 2008.

Oliver Stönner-Venkatarama, an emerging market analyst at Commerzbank, said it was no surprise that the Czech Republic was facing budget problems. "They're under pressure because of the labor market," he said.

There are a few success stories. Estonia, with low inflation and almost no debt, has made "amazing" progress, according to Mr. Issing. It already pegs its currency to the euro, and could probably adopt the currency without disruption, analysts say.

But critics say that Europe's demand for fiscal discipline is ringing hollow at a time when 5 of the 12 euro countries—including the two largest, Germany and France—are in violation of the deficit rules.

Mr. Trichet said the situation led to an "obvious" question regarding the deteriorating fiscal situation of the would-be members. If Germany and France do not abide by the rules, why should other countries?

Still, the new countries have shown little sign of trying to use the Germans and the French as an alibi for their own fiscal problems. Analysts say these countries recognize that they have to meet the requirements to get into the club before they can question the club's rules.

The bigger issue, some experts said, is that the race to adopt the euro has become less urgent for most countries. They are struggling with thorny problems, like chronic unemployment, inflation, and bankrupt pension systems, which a new currency will not solve.

"It wouldn't be in the interest of these countries to be in the euro zone right now," said Katinka Barysch, the chief economist at the Center for European Reform in London. "It's not their main priority."

Europe's Society Under Strain, Says Leaked Economic Report

By Richard Carter
EUOBSERVER.COM, October 18, 2004

The EU's economic targets for 2010 are set to be seriously missed, according to a draft of a long-awaited competitiveness report, obtained by the EUobserver.

The hard-hitting document which assesses the EU's position in its bid to become the most competitive, knowledge-based economy in the world by 2010 (known as the Lisbon Agenda) warns that "too many targets promise to be seriously missed."

To be officially presented to EU leaders next month, the draft report foresees devastating effects if the Lisbon process is not invigorated.

"What is at risk . . . is nothing less than the sustainability of the society Europe has built and to that extent, the viability of its civilisation," says the paper, drawn up by 13 experts led by former Dutch prime minister Wim Kok.

The working population will be unable to sustain "Europe's growing army of pensioners," economic growth will "stagnate," and institutions face "contraction and decline."

"In sum, Europe has lost ground to both the U.S. and Asia; its societies are under strain; and some ugly political forces are beginning to manifest themselves," is the gloomy conclusion of the 37-page draft.

Enlargement to Make Things Harder

While the enlargement of the EU to 25 member states is described as "a welcome expansion," it has "made European-wide achievement of the Lisbon goals even harder."

The new member states have lower employment rates and productivity levels, making it more difficult for the EU to catch up with the U.S. in these respects.

However, the rapid growth of the new member states is "a positive aspect of enlargement . . . creating an area of economic dynamism in East Europe," says the report.

Many—including some finance ministers—have proposed that the deadline of 2010 be pushed back to allow the EU more time to achieve its goals.

But the report rejects this unequivocally and urges ambition in the EU's aims. "Should the 2010 deadline be lifted? Again no."

"Lisbon should not be regarded as a one-off objective to be disregarded after 2010 even if every target had been achieved; rather it is an ongoing process aimed at securing Europe's future as a high productivity, high value-added, high employment economy."

Don't Copy the U.S.

Although the EU is aiming to catch up with the U.S., it should not aim to "become a copy-cat U.S.—far from it," recommends the report.

"Europe has made its own distinctive choices about the social model that it wants to retain; whether life expectancy, infant mortality rates, income inequality, or poverty, Europe has a better record than the U.S. and wants to preserve and improve."

However, the authors of the text concede that "Lisbon is not a picture of unrelieved gloom, as some like to paint."

Since the launch of the Lisbon process, over 6 million jobs have been created, whereas the employment rate in the U.S. has fallen.

But the EU-15 still needs to create 11 million new jobs by 2010 if it is to succeed in its target of having a 70 percent employment rate by this time.

More Innovation, Please

The report recommends, amongst other things, an increase in innovation, harmonisation of the way corporate tax is calculated, and cutting red tape for businesses.

But the message to EU leaders is clear: "halfway to 2010, the overall picture is very mixed and much needs to be done in order to prevent Lisbon from becoming a synonym for missed objectives and failed promises."

Beyond Integration

Squaring Europe's Social Preferences with Robust Growth

BY MICHAEL DEPPLER
FINANCE & DEVELOPMENT, JUNE 2004

Ten new members joined the European Union (EU) on May 1 in the biggest enlargement of the community since its inception. Just 15 years after the fall of the Berlin Wall, eight Central and Eastern European countries joined, along with Cyprus and Malta, expanding the EU's membership by two-thirds, its land area by a fourth, and its population by a fifth (to over 450 million). This latest step in European integration is expected to further help cement peace and promote prosperity throughout the continent. But the occasion is clouded by the considerable misgivings in Europe and elsewhere about the EU's ability to adjust to changing economic circumstances.

The core economic concern is the weak growth performance of Europe—and particularly of the 12 countries at the epicenter of European integration that use the euro as their common currency—relative to the rest of the world and especially the United States. Underlying this concern are the problems of sagging long-term trends in the growth of productivity, the use of labor resources, and—looking forward—the dwindling size of the workforce because of population aging.

But these structural worries gain immediacy from fears about the short term as well. With the euro area still just emerging from a prolonged slowdown and seemingly dependent on exports for growth, the euro having appreciated steeply against the U.S. dollar, and the U.S. current account deficit at 5 percent of GDP, prospects for the global as well as the European economy rest to a large extent on whether Europe can improve its domestically generated growth performance. Adding weight to these concerns are the perceptions that the euro area's fiscal and monetary policies are excessively oriented toward preserving medium-term stability and insufficiently focused on sustaining demand in the short term. In tandem with continuing concerns about the implication of aging populations for long-term growth and fiscal sustainability, tensions stemming from immigration, and international criticism of the high levels of protection afforded to agriculture, it is clear that enlargement has occurred at a time of considerable doubt and misgiving about the integration enterprise.

To gain some perspective on these issues, it is useful to step back and look at the broad sweep of Europe's postwar economic history. This article seeks to provide a framework for understanding the main issue—whether and how the core EU social and economic model can deliver robust growth, or whether attaining robust growth requires adaptation of the European model. Looking forward, such a perspective suggests that prospects are neither as bleak as observers sometimes think nor as rosy as European policy choices might suggest.

Europe's Twin Impulses

Although many factors played a role, postwar developments can be viewed as reflecting two broad-based, ebbing and flowing, and sometimes contrary impulses: toward social solidarity and equity, on the one hand, and financial discipline and economic efficiency, on the other. The historical roots of these preferences run deep.

Prospects are neither as bleak as observers sometimes think nor as rosy as European policy choices might suggest.

The solidarity dimension stems from a widely shared desire for social peace and cohesion, with roots in the welfare policies inherited from the late 19th century, the political and social upheavals of the first half of the 20th century that culminated in World War II, and the relative homogeneity of Europe's populations. The discipline dimension, perhaps surprisingly, seems to have similar roots. Most cited is the case of Germany, where the deep desire for economic stability can be traced back to the devastating hyperinflation of the early 1920s. These twin impulses led many countries to develop increasingly generous pay-as-you-go social insurance systems—systems that took care of social spending within a disciplined, self-financing framework. Along the way, continental Europe's corporatist traditions, topped by various forms of "social partnership," cemented the structure, for good or ill, through all echelons of society.

These preferences still obtain today. Fundamentally, continental Europe is committed to a financially disciplined welfare state. Robust growth is on everyone's agenda, as exemplified by the call at the EU summit in Lisbon in March 2000 to turn Europe into "the world's most dynamic and competitive economy." But the quest for growth is also where the differences emerge. To put it simply: can growth best be achieved through discipline (and more supply-oriented approaches that would require adapting the social model) or through solidarity (and approaches that might require, if not a loosening of financial discipline, more spending)? While the differences are fundamental, the two sides are careful not to question, at least loudly, the core value of the other: the welfare state and financial discipline. The reason is simple: a combination of the two has been the revealed preference of the electorate for decades and remains so today. Hence, the general tenor of economic policies has been to call for both, as the Lisbon Declaration does.

Momentum Toward Integration

Solidarity and discipline have propelled European integration throughout the postwar period, with solidarity as the stepping-stone. On the heels of two disastrous world wars, it provided the momentum for removing barriers and raising living standards through convergence in per capita incomes—a process known as real convergence. In this respect, the EU's beginnings are traceable to the European Coal and Steel Community, set up in 1952. This led to two further milestones of real convergence: the Treaty of Rome (1957), which established the European Economic Community (a customs union with common external tariffs and a common agricultural policy); and the Single European Act (1986), which committed all members to creating a single EU market for goods, services, capital, and labor.

In time, this impulse toward European integration was balanced by more discipline, perhaps most evident in the institutional developments designed to ensure price and financial stability throughout the Union—so-called nominal convergence. Initially, discipline was provided by the Bretton Woods exchange rate system. But its breakdown in the early 1970s set off a scramble for a new nominal anchor,

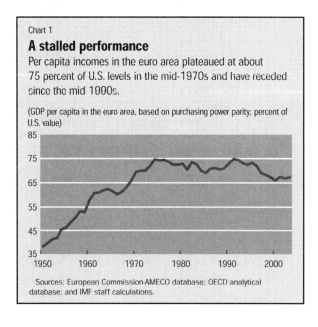

Chart 1

A stalled performance

Per capita incomes in the euro area plateaued at about 75 percent of U.S. levels in the mid-1970s and have receded since the mid 1990s.

(GDP per capita in the euro area, based on purchasing power parity; percent of U.S. value)

Sources: European Commission-AMECO database; OECD analytical database; and IMF staff calculations.

which culminated, in the late 1970s, in the European Monetary System. The exchange rate mechanism (ERM) of this system constrained exchange rate fluctuations among the participating countries, with Germany emerging as the undisputed nominal anchor country. However, continued nominal divergences and the associated pressures on exchange rates within the ERM high-

> *Integration has been a major source of European growth.*

lighted the need for more convergence of macroeconomic policies. Matters were brought to a head in the early 1990s when the liberalization of capital movements and German unification prompted the 1992 crisis in the ERM, hastening the ratification of the Maastricht Treaty and the road map for Economic and Monetary Union (EMU). Besides exchange rate criteria, potential member countries were now obliged to meet other nominal convergence criteria as well, particularly for inflation, fiscal deficits, and government debt. The treaty's fiscal provisions were later fleshed out in regulations known as the Stability and Growth Pact (SGP). At the beginning of 1999, 11 EMU members irrevocably fixed their exchange rates and adopted the euro as their single currency, and the newly constituted European Central Bank (ECB) took on the task of conducting a single monetary policy for the euro area.

The impulse to deeper economic integration was accompanied by a like-spirited widening of its reach as the EU expanded by leaps and bounds—a process set to continue even after the latest enlargement round. The European Coal and Steel Community comprised six countries in the heart of Europe (Belgium, France, Germany, Italy, Luxembourg, and Netherlands). Successive waves of enlargements in 1973 (Ireland, Denmark, and United Kingdom), 1981 (Greece), 1986 (Portugal and Spain), and 1995 (Austria, Finland, and Sweden) boosted EU membership to 15 countries by the time plans for EMU had gelled into an operational blueprint. With the latest expansion on May 1 of this year, the EU family has grown to 25 countries with considerable economic and cultural diversity—a diversity that will only increase. Bulgaria and Romania are well advanced in their negotiations and are set to join in the next few years. Decisions on the timing of Turkey's negotiations are also pending. The states of the Western Balkans are next in line, with Croatia's application already given the green light by the EU Commission. In a step that reaches beyond integration, the EU's "Wider Europe Neighborhood" initiative encompasses 14 countries to its east and south and aims to develop a "ring of friends" with which the EU desires to have peaceful and cooperative relations on the basis of shared values. Iceland, Norway, and Switzerland remain outside the EU.

Integration has been a major source of European growth. It was part and parcel of Europe's rapid real convergence with the United States during much of the postwar period, with the creation of the common market being widely credited as having significantly boosted intra-area trade and regional growth. Indeed, the evidence points to further positive trade effects in the euro area following the establishment of EMU. Moreover, despite earlier fears to the contrary, trade with non-EU countries has, over time, also increased. In the same vein, promotion of nominal convergence—particularly through the Maastricht criteria and the establishment of EMU—engendered a disciplining of fiscal and monetary policies, a convergence of inflation back to low single digits throughout Europe, and, for a while at least, a spurt of reforms among most future members. Indeed, by the 1990s, the EU had deservedly become a beacon throughout Eastern Europe for sound macroeconomic policies and aspirations for higher levels of real income, as well as democracy, solidarity, and human rights: becoming a member of the club became the priority of governments and one that enabled them to muster the popular support needed to overcome the challenges of transition.

Waning Growth

While integration spurred higher growth, in good part by inducing change at the national level, its positive effects were gradually supplanted by the less benign effects of domestic rigidities.

It did not start out that way. During the early years, Europe's model effectively delivered on all counts: social cohesion, financial discipline, and rapid growth. Real convergence toward U.S. levels was seemingly effortless in the first three decades of the postwar period, as incomes, employment, investment, consumption, and wealth spiraled upward in a virtuous circle. Convergence was fostered, in part, by the externally imposed discipline of the Bretton Woods system and the relatively good inflation and financial performances associated with it.

The next three decades proved difficult, however. The combination of two large oil shocks, an increasingly generous welfare system, and unrealistic income expectations built up during the period of rapid catch-up growth together with the financial indiscipline associated with the breakdown of the Bretton Woods framework resulted in marked macroeconomic instability and imbalances. Indeed, experiments with activist Keynesian stabilization policies during the 1970s were unsuccessful, and such policies became discredited, particularly in Germany. In the end, the system reverted to the paradigm. It protected the jobs and real incomes of those already employed, but it also reasserted financial discipline by increasingly accepting the German mark as its anchor. The outcome was large increases in labor taxation that ultimately undermined employment but stimulated investment. This strengthened labor productivity and preserved the competitiveness of those with jobs.

With unemployment trending upward, the system adjusted further. Wage moderation together with measures to lower the cost of labor and relax labor market restrictions, particularly for new entrants to the job market, yielded hefty increases in employment from the mid-1990s. And the Maastricht Treaty, EMU, the ECB, and the SGP became the successors to the German mark in providing financial discipline.

Overall, however, Europe's performance remained unenviable. Per capita incomes remained stuck at about 75 percent of U.S. levels up to the mid-1990s, with rapid increases in labor productivity being offset by weakness in employment. Per capita incomes later slipped to close to two-thirds of U.S. levels as productivity growth sagged in Europe and accelerated in the United States in the second half of the 1990s. Negative perceptions of this lackluster performance of the euro area were compounded by even larger, and better-known, differences in GDP growth stemming from transatlantic differences in population growth.

Too Much Stability and Discipline?

The slowing of growth is often ascribed in good part to the EU's (or the euro area's) "stability bias," that is, its unwillingness to engage in countercyclical demand management policies, which would involve boosting demand (through lower interest rates and larger fiscal deficits) when growth is weak and dampening demand (through higher interest rates and smaller fiscal deficits or surpluses) when it is strong. As suggested earlier, Europe's macroeconomic policy frameworks do indeed spring in considerable measure from the impulse toward discipline, that is to say, from a will to contain what is viewed as the cumulation of monetary and fiscal risks—ultimately pernicious to growth—associated with unrestrained political and social processes. Since the 1970s, in particular, the emphasis has been on establishing and preserving medium-term stability and not on managing aggregate demand in the short run through countercyclical policies. This bent is clear from the ECB's Maastricht Treaty mandate: "the primary objective . . . shall be to maintain price stability." It is also clear from the treaty's provisions on ensuring sound government finances: "Member states shall avoid excessive government deficits," where compliance with this commandment is assessed relative to reference values of 3 percent of GDP for the fiscal deficit and 60 percent for the debt-to-GDP ratio.

This manifest emphasis on stability tends to prompt misunderstandings about macroeconomic policies. Criticism that European institutions are insufficiently mindful of cyclical considerations falls on deaf ears. This leads observers to think that the criticisms are even more justified than initially thought. And the fact that policies have, in practice, been fairly sensitive to the economic cycle gets lost amid the din. This gap between rhetoric and reality has beset both the ECB and the SGP.

In this vein, the ECB is criticized for taking insufficient account of cyclical conditions in setting interest rates, to which it responds that this is to misunderstand its mission. Its mantra has consistently been price stability now and forever. In fact, however, it has largely behaved like an inflation targeter, mindful of the implications of growth for inflation. This gets overlooked, in part, because the rhetoric prompts the mistaken assumption that the ECB is facing the same kind of economy as the U.S. Federal Reserve. In fact, at least partly because of the welfare element of Europe's paradigm, the ECB has faced considerably smaller output gaps (and employment volatility) and markedly more persistent inflation than the Federal Reserve. The rhetoric has tended to mask the fact that the differences in policies mostly reflect these different conditions.

The contrast between European and U.S. approaches to macroeconomic policies remains.

The same duality between rhetoric and reality applies to the SGP. The pact is widely criticized as a deficient countercyclical policy instrument. This is hardly surprising since its legal core is plainly aimed at defining limits and not at defining countercyclical policies within those limits. The fact that these limits are specified in terms of actual (rather than cyclically adjusted) fiscal balances lends additional weight to the criticism that the pact is procyclical; it appears to require that deficits be reduced when they are being widened by the effects of weak growth, with resulting contractionary effects on the economy, and vice versa.

However, the fact is that fiscal policies under the SGP have been significantly less procyclical than they were in the aftermath of what is now viewed as the Keynesian misadventures of the 1970s. Indeed, widespread perceptions to the contrary notwithstanding, for the euro area as a whole, fiscal policies since the introduction of the euro have generally allowed full play to the so-called automatic stabilizers—that is, the fiscal mechanisms (like income taxes and unemployment benefits) that automatically dampen cyclical swings by boosting demand when the economy slumps (because tax receipts fall) and curbing demand when inflationary pressures build (because tax receipts rise). This is significant because the differences in the size of government in the economy imply that the automatic stabilizers are about twice as large in Europe as in the United States.

The situation is further complicated by the de facto evolution of Europe's policy frameworks over the past few years toward more cyclically attuned approaches. One example is the gradual narrowing of the ECB's definition of price stability from 0–2 percent to, in effect, 1–2 percent and, most recently, to "close to but below 2 percent" inflation. Another is the gradual acceptance of the role of the automatic fiscal stabilizers, of estimates of cyclically adjusted balances to measure the underlying fiscal position, and of the objective of achieving underlying balance in the medium term in SGP-linked assessments of fiscal policies. The system is seeking solutions that twin discipline with good demand management policies.

That said, the contrast between European and U.S. approaches to macroeconomic policies remains: the Europeans take a more medium-term view, in good part because the welfare system (solidarity) protects those adversely affected by the vicissitudes of the cycle; the United States is more proactive in securing short-run growth and employment, in good part because there is less such protection. Given these differences in structure, comparative assessments of macroeconomic policies need to focus more on growth and inflation outcomes than on the cyclical shifts in policy stance. In that regard, it may be noted that, measured in terms of the cyclical volatility of output or employment, Europe's performance is comparable to, if not better than, that of the United States. Perceptions to the contrary mainly reflect something more enduring: the longer-term weakening of growth in Europe.

Unaffordable Solidarity?

Many view Europe's weakening growth as a reflection of its overly generous welfare arrangements, which, by muffling incentives to work and protecting businesses and workers from the disciplines of competition, have exacted an inordinate cost in terms of per capita incomes. In this view, this has led to large-scale underutilization of labor resources and slowed incorporation of new technologies and adjustment to shifting sources of comparative advantage.

The reality is more mixed. Europe has undertaken many reforms over the years, some of which have begun to pay off. Many have been designed to strengthen the demand side of the labor market,

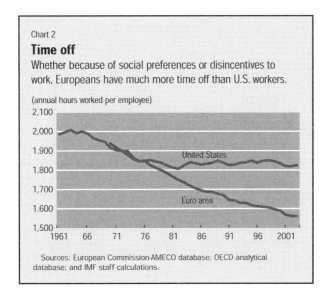

Chart 2

Time off

Whether because of social preferences or disincentives to work, Europeans have much more time off than U.S. workers.

(annual hours worked per employee)

Sources: European Commission-AMECO database; OECD analytical database; and IMF staff calculations.

in the form of either wage moderation and other measures to lower the cost of labor or measures that make labor markets more flexible and encourage new entrants. In the same vein, the single market initiative sought to combat "eurosclerosis" by setting in motion deep and wide-ranging reforms in product and financial markets. These reforms continue to run their course. The resulting increase in competition is boosting efficiency, including in the use of labor in those markets.

These policies have achieved more than is often recognized. The euro area generated almost 10 million jobs between 1997 and 2003, 2 million more than the United States. Although the surge in employment has slowed productivity growth, this could reflect transitional adjustment problems. The payoff to reforms often takes decades, not years, to accrue, and Europe's employment performance should continue to improve. The uneven distribution of growth across Europe is also noteworthy. It has been especially weak in Germany, the country where labor market reforms have been most delayed. Elsewhere, growth and employment have

---

Differences in per capita incomes exist between the United States and virtually every EU country.

---

tended to be more robust. Indeed, they have been strongest in the smaller, more open economies, partly because the interaction of solidarity and discipline has led to more encompassing and proactive policies in these countries. This is also true of the Scandinavian countries, which have the strongest welfare systems.

Nevertheless, differences in per capita incomes exist between the United States and virtually every EU country, and the larger issue is whether they reflect excessive solidarity or a "social choice"—that is, a willingness to forgo higher per capita incomes for certain social goals, such as increased leisure. About half of the difference between U.S. and European per capita incomes is tied to the fact that Europeans work fewer hours per person: about 1,500 hours a year versus 1,800 in the United States. Many observers in Europe view this as a preference for leisure over work at the going wage. A contrary view, which starts from the observation that annual working hours in the United States and Europe were the same 30 years ago, is that the current gap reflects the large disincentives to work imposed over the past 30 years, implicitly in an attempt to "share" employment. With Europe about to shift from an era of a plentiful supply of workers to one of a dwindling labor supply because of aging, growth prospects hinge in part on who is right and whether incentives, if they are important, will be changed.

Be this as it may, change is in the offing, partly because there is a will to be better prepared for the effects of globalization and new technologies. Change will also be necessitated by the economics of aging populations and discipline. Without change, fiscal policies in many countries are on an unsustainable course, with public debt ratios rising steeply. If nothing else, therefore, the desire for financial discipline should again force adjustment. What remains open, however, is whether the adjustment will enhance growth. Many governments have chosen to deal with aging not by streamlining the welfare system but by shifting budgets into surplus. This reduces the interest payable on the public debt, making governments better able to afford the coming increases in public spending on pensions and health without undermining the fiscal position. The approach, very much in the tradition of the financially disciplined welfare state, leaves incentive systems unchanged, however, and does little to improve future growth prospects.

Looking Ahead

With solidarity and discipline seen as the keystones of Europe's postwar economic history, the continent may be viewed as still seeking to bring them into greater harmony. One must applaud the inclusiveness of the EU, which solidarity has fostered. But one must regret the protection of stakeholders, the slow adjustment to change, and the slowing of growth, with the resulting periodic "dashes for growth" or unaffordable tax cuts that it also encourages. In contrast, discipline and the hard times that made it binding have provided a constructive antidote, fostering necessary changes and reforms. These should lead to improvements in performance in the coming years. But the discipline has too often been in the form of limits (initially on the exchange rate and now, more loosely, on fiscal policies). The resulting policy adjustments have thus tended to be reactive, asymmetric, and insufficiently forward-looking, particularly in the larger countries.

The implications of these tensions for short-term demand management policies are relatively slight. While the rhetoric reaches its apogee in downturns, as it has recently, the reality is that—particularly if one accepts the importance of discipline in keeping to a reasonable, long-term course—fiscal and monetary policies have generally been appropriate in dealing with the cyclical component of downturns. If there is a short-term demand management problem, it is rather in the absence of discipline at cyclical peaks when repressed solidarity-bred instincts gain momentum. But these problems affect, in the first instance, the short-run volatility of growth, not its trend rate.

The implications for the long term are more significant: here, the unresolved tensions between solidarity and discipline remain deeply problematic, particularly at the national level. Because of solidarity-based tendencies to preserve the status quo, electorates resist forward-looking reforms and insist on tangible, direct, and immediate evidence of a problem before accepting that it should be addressed. Hence, the approach to reforms tends to be partial and episodic even though deep, forward-looking, and increasingly politically difficult reforms are widely seen to be necessary if growth is to be robust.

Thus, while past reforms may ultimately improve performance in the years ahead, growth is still likely to disappoint, and discipline and bad times are still likely to remain an essential spur to reform. Indeed, if the foregoing analysis is anywhere near the mark, obituaries for the SGP are missing the point. While adjustments to the SGP are likely in the light of experience, an essential core aimed at constraining political and social pressures via budgets should and will remain.

But discipline-induced structural adjustment is not the best option. Instead, what is needed is a more forward-looking and thoroughgoing approach to reform whereby solidarity and discipline are reconciled through policies that generate higher long-term growth. This is not impossible. Some of the smaller countries have achieved a measure of success this way. Moreover, at the continental level, European integration is testimony to the generous, forward-looking dimensions of the solidarity impulse. However, achieving thoroughgoing reform at the national level—particularly in the larger economies—will require skill (and perhaps some luck). But most of all, it will require a willingness by policymakers and the electorates to look beyond the current election cycle.

EU Offers to Eliminate Its Farm Export Subsidies at World Trade Talks, But Only If U.S., Canada, Japan Follow

By Constant Brand
Associated Press, May 10, 2004

Aiming to boost world trade talks, the European Union offered Monday to drop billions of dollars in subsidies on farm exports—but only if the United States, Japan, Canada, and other rich nations make similar concessions.

EU trade commissioner Pascal Lamy said the EU was ready to "go the extra mile" to get a midterm deal by July at the World Trade Organization.

"We are ready to show flexibility," Lamy told reporters. "Everything is on the list, everything is on the table."

But he added a further dismantling of EU export subsidies would depend on a "mutual disarmament" from other key agricultural exporters like the United States, Australia, and Canada.

U.S. trade representative Robert B. Zoellick in Washington welcomed the EU announcement and expressed cautious optimism about prospects for a deal.

"We are beginning to see the shape of a foundation upon which to build in the coming weeks and months," he said.

With a key WTO ministerial meeting on Thursday in Paris, Lamy and EU agriculture commissioner Franz Fischler sent a letter to all 147 members of the WTO outlining three areas where the 25-nation trade giant was willing to compromise.

It said the EU would cut "all export subsidies" on condition Washington and others do the same with their farm support programs.

The EU wants Washington to do away with subsidized export credits on farm products, and the practice of buying farm surpluses to provide food aid for poor countries.

It also pointed to Canada's monopolistic marketing of crops through its wheat board, which regulates production and prices.

"Our American, Australian, or Canadian partners have to make clear that they will fully match the EU on the forms of export support they use," said EU farm commissioner Franz Fischler.

Zoellick noted Washington "already offered to eliminate U.S. export subsidies" and would agree to negotiate "a parallel elimination of the subsidy element within export credits, and to negotiate disciplines on food aid to preclude displacement of commercial sales.

"We look to others to show a similar spirit by stating their willingness to end monopolies in state trading enterprises and differential export taxes," he added.

Lamy also suggested a special trade package for the WTO's 90 poorest members and expressed willingness to compromise on other issues, including competition rules, investment, and government procurement policies.

With elections in the United States looming in November, and the current European Commission term set to expire in October, Lamy said it was time to push ahead at the Paris meeting.

"We have a window of opportunity which a number of us want to

---

Agriculture is the major stumbling block in the WTO trade round, which is already months behind schedule.

---

take advantage of," Lamy said. "We want to be more open, simpler, and clearer."

Agriculture is the major stumbling block in the WTO trade round, which is already months behind schedule. WTO members have set themselves a deadline of July to agree on the framework for negotiations, including the formula for tackling agricultural tariffs.

The so-called Group of 20 developing countries, led by Brazil, South Africa, and India, have long demanded the EU and the United States get rid of what they see as unfair subsidies.

Lamy said the EU has already moved to slash export subsidies to 3 billion euros ($3.5 billion) a year from as much as 15 billion euros a year over a decade ago.

The international relief organization Oxfam called for the EU to act unilaterally and set an example.

"If the EU is serious about showing real leadership in a genuine development round, these concessions should not be made conditional on progress in market access and domestic support, and should not require reciprocal action by the U.S.," said Jo Leadbetter from Oxfam.

Old Continent, New Deal

By Martha Neil
ABA Journal, September 2004

The evolution of the European Union is changing the political
and economic landscape of the continent. Indeed, the creation and
growth of the EU may be the most profound development in
Europe's history that wasn't accompanied by conquest and war.
And the legal repercussions of what's happening in Europe are
being felt in the United States.

A unified Europe has long been the dream of both dictators and
idealists, but it took the trauma of World War II to trigger serious
efforts to bring some unity to the disparate national political structures, monetary systems, and cultures on the continent. Those
efforts were bolstered by the growth of democratic governments in
Western Europe following the war, and later by the collapse of the
Soviet bloc in the east.

Now the European Union spans the continent and boasts one of
the world's most powerful economies. In May, 10 nations, most of
them formerly in the Soviet bloc, officially joined the EU, bringing
its membership to 25 nations with a total population of nearly 500
million people—200-plus million more than the population of the
United States.

The EU's unofficial boundaries reach from the Republic of Ireland and the United Kingdom in the west, to Poland and the Baltic
States in the east, to Greece and across the Mediterranean Sea to
Italy, Spain, and Portugal. Bulgaria, Romania, and perhaps Turkey are expected to join within the next few years.

And by its own account, the European Union is unique. It is not
designed to replace Europe's existing nations. Rather, its members
have adopted a form of "integration" under which they delegate
some of their sovereignty to common institutions, including a parliament, courts, and financial agencies, that decide political and
economic matters of joint interest.

Some of those concessions of sovereignty have been significant.
On Jan. 1, 2002, a dozen EU nations, including France and Ger-
many, replaced their own currencies with the euro. (The United
Kingdom is the most notable holdout.) And a convention is writing

a constitution for the EU that will address issues concerning individual rights as well as government structure and economic cooperation.

Far-Reaching Impact

A burgeoning behemoth like the European Union is bound to make waves, and they're washing up on U.S. shores with increasing frequency and impact. After all, Europe is still the major trading partner for U.S. businesses. Moreover, the EU is quickly developing a body of law that is having a significant impact on American companies doing business in Europe, even as it diverges in some key ways from U.S. law.

In an increasingly global legal environment, U.S. lawyers will have no choice but to take notice when uniform laws and standard legal practices are established for such a large number of countries, say experts in the field. That creates opportunities, as well as obstacles, for U.S. lawyers representing clients who do business in Europe.

"All these great issues!" exclaims Lawrence M. Gill of Chicago. The current climate "is of great benefit, I think, to savvy lawyers who

---

A burgeoning behemoth like the European Union is bound to make waves.

---

can look a little bit into the future and prepare their clients for these significant changes," says Gill, a member of the council of the ABA Section of International Law and Practice.

"Any time you have a change that impacts as many states as there are now in the EU," says Gill, "it's going to have an impact on the United States."

Citing just one example, Gill says an EU mandate that all its member states start using international financial reporting standards as of Jan. 1 will create a tremendous amount of potential work for U.S. lawyers.

The new financial reporting standards will become the EU's version of the Generally Accepted Accounting Principles that are routinely used by U.S. companies for annual reports, audits, and other financial documents.

At first glance, it might seem that adopting the international standards would be of interest primarily to accountants, but Gill says different auditing standards can lead to huge variances in a company's reportable income and amount of debt. If so, a wide range of transactions, from mergers and acquisitions to existing loan agreements, may have to be reconsidered by U.S. companies or their subsidiaries doing business with European counterparts. U.S. lawyers also will have to monitor the possible merger of the two sets of standards, he says.

The sudden shift to international standards throughout the European Union on Jan. 1 "will have a significant impact on the documents, and transactional and contractual relationships that U.S. companies enter into," says Gill, even in some cases for companies that don't do much business overseas.

"Eurojargon"

At least in the view of many lawyers on this side of the pond, one of the more dubious achievements of the European Union has been to bring administrative law to new levels of complexity.

Perhaps that shouldn't be surprising in light of what the EU is trying to accomplish by synchronizing the economic regulatory structures of 25 separate member states to encourage freer trade among EU members and a more united approach to dealing with outside markets.

But in practice, the European Union is building a layer of oversight that in some cases defers to the national laws of its member states and in some cases trumps them, and often requires member states to find ways to implement EU laws and regulations.

One of the more dubious achievements of the European Union has been to bring administrative law to new levels of complexity.

For the uninitiated, things are made even more difficult by the web of regulatory agencies based in various EU locales and the proliferation of arcane terminology—dubbed "Eurojargon"—in which those agencies immerse their pronouncements. Even the EU itself acknowledges the problem by including an extensive glossary on its Web site, *www.europa.eu.int.*

"My own personal judgment is that it has added a significant layer of complexity," says Stanley J. Marcuss, a Washington, D.C., lawyer, of the EU's regulatory structure.

"Many of the national laws in Europe have remained on the books" at the same time that a new regulatory layer has been imposed by the EU, says Marcuss. "In any significant way, I don't think it has smoothed the way to removing regulatory and trade barriers."

Erika Christian Collins, an employment lawyer in New York City, reaches a similar conclusion.

"In the EU, the directives come down and then the member states have to promulgate regulations," says Collins, a vice chair of the International Employment Law Committee in the international law section. "I think data privacy is a perfect example of this, because the member state regulations are all very different in terms of getting down to the letter of the law and complying. It's a big challenge for U.S. companies, because a lot of U.S. companies are in several or even all the [EU] member countries, and they've got to do something a little bit different in each member state."

There have, certainly, been a number of instances in which the EU's regulatory structure has had a streamlining effect, say American experts.

One example is the "community trademark," which offers one-stop shopping to protect a mark throughout the EU, says Madison, Wis., attorney Gina G. Carter. "Most people who want to do business in Europe are not just targeting one country," she notes. "So the community trademark is very useful."

But another international law expert cautions American practitioners to be prepared for more changes in the EU's legal and regulatory structure. That structure "is not complete," says George A. Bermann, a law professor at Columbia University in New York City. "There are directives and things being added all the time."

Bermann is director of a project initiated by the ABA Section of Administrative Law and Regulatory Practice earlier this year to help U.S. lawyers navigate the unfamiliar and shifting waters of EU law and regulation.

The primary goal of the project is to produce a statement that sets forth the general principles and practices that govern the EU's administrative law, according to a project outline that Bermann submitted in February to the administrative law section's council. Background reports will provide more detailed discussion of various aspects of EU administrative law.

The areas covered by the statement and background reports will include adjudication, rule-making, judicial review, transparency (access to information on the rule-making process), data protection, and oversight of the administrative process.

The project is slated for completion in 2006. The final product should be broadly similar to a statement of federal administrative law in the United States, according to Bermann's report. That statement was produced in 2002, and one of the background reports has been published while work continues on the others.

The need for an effort like that being initiated by the administrative law section helps to illustrate a continuing reality for American lawyers representing clients on matters in Europe or anywhere else beyond U.S. borders: Other legal systems are likely to handle things differently, and American lawyers operating on foreign turf are going to have to adjust to those different approaches.

For instance, the administrative process being developed by the European Union still reflects a general approach common to its member states but dissimilar to the U.S. system. The EU's administrative law system is not governed by statutes that can be referred to for explanations of the regulatory scheme, says William F. Funk, the outgoing chair of the administrative law section.

And the notice-and-comment rule-making so integral to U.S. administrative law has no significant role in the EU administrative process, says Funk, a law professor at Lewis & Clark College in Portland, Ore. Instead, the EU bases the transparency of its processes for developing administrative rules on making documents public.

In addition, Funk and other experts say the administrative process in Europe is not as formalized as the U.S. system, which means that more is accomplished through personal dealings with officers of administrative agencies.

As a result, Funk says, U.S. lawyers who don't have a lot of on-the-ground presence in Brussels, where most EU government agencies are headquartered, may be working at something of a disadvantage.

"For most American law firms and most American businesses that don't on a daily basis have dealing with the EU, it's pretty much a black box," says Funk. "It's not like it's secret. It's just that you're not part of the process."

Talk to Those in the Know

Contrary to U.S. practice, transactional matters of any complexity in the EU tend to be handled in informal negotiations, says T. Andrew Ragusin, who worked in Brussels for a U.S. law firm and now serves as European counsel to a number of American companies.

"I think that going in cold is a big mistake," says Ragusin. "I think you need to talk to people who have a lot of experience, who know the players, and who can direct you to the right individual or individuals."

The assistance of experienced counsel is crucial, says Ragusin. "If you have any questions at all," he says, "the smart money is on liaising with commission officials," and resolving the issues collaboratively.

His reference is to the European Commission, the EU's primary administrative agency with rule-making authority. It was the commission, for instance, that ruled against Microsoft in March in a claim that the software giant had violated European competition laws.

The commission fined Microsoft a record $497 million euros (roughly $613 million) on grounds that the Redmond, Wash.–based company sells its software in Europe in a way that violates the EU's competition rules. The commission maintained that the changes it ordered Microsoft to make will improve competition in the software field on a global basis.

In June, the EU agreed to lift the order until the European Court of Justice, the EU's highest judicial body, considers an appeal by Microsoft.

Meanwhile, the U.S. Circuit Court of Appeals for the District of Columbia in June approved a settlement between Microsoft and the Justice Department in a similar antitrust suit. The settlement includes provisions that will allow consumers to more easily use software from companies competing with Microsoft on computers that use Microsoft's Windows program.

Antitrust is an area that highlights the different regulatory styles of the United States and the European Union. It also illustrates their varying approaches to managing the competitive instincts of companies, as well as how the laws of each reach into other jurisdictions.

Even when a merger involves only U.S. companies, EU antitrust law can be implicated if the companies have significant connections to Europe, says Ragusin. And whenever that is the case, he adds, it's important to begin informal negotiations with EU officials early in the process to address antitrust issues.

This is a common approach in Europe, he says, but U.S. lawyers accustomed to resolving antitrust issues in a more formal setting often fail to recognize it. And that could cause a merger sanctioned by U.S. authorities to fail due to lack of approval from counterparts in the EU.

Moreover, Ragusin says, a "philosophical gulf" exists between American and European Union antitrust regulators. The U.S. Department of Justice and the Federal Trade Commission routinely focus on potential harm to consumers in evaluating a prospective merger. EU regulators, on the other hand, are concerned primarily about adverse effects the merger will have on competitors.

Those different approaches have come close to scuttling mergers of U.S. corporations on recent occasions, notes Ragusin.

In 2000, for instance, a merger of General Electric (an airplane engine manufacturer) and Honeywell (which makes avionics and aircraft components) was vetoed by EU regulators after the U.S. Justice Department approved it. Justice accepted the companies' argument that the combination would result in a more efficient operation leading to lower prices for consumers. The EU, however, saw a potential for unfair competition.

Another example involves two U.S. companies that had no assets or subsidiaries in Europe. But the EU had jurisdiction over the attempted merger of McDonnell-Douglas and Boeing (both manufacturers of commercial airplanes and components) because of their sales to European airlines.

The FTC approved the merger on grounds that it would not substantially reduce competition due to Boeing's preexisting market dominance. The EU, however, decided that the merger would significantly enhance Boeing's market lead. It took years after the companies began trying to merge in 1997 to gain the EU's approval, Ragusin recounts.

Several treaties have encouraged cooperation between EU and American antitrust regulators, with some success, but more efforts are needed to integrate the two systems, says Ragusin.

"While these agreements have been successful at the enforcement level, they have failed to foster a cooperative climate in the clearance of transactions such as the GE/Honeywell and the Boeing/McDonnell-Douglas mergers," he says. Thus, "Renewed calls for a more collaborative effort between the two sets of regulators were made this spring, given the serious economic and financial repercussions of the philosophical divide."

In another area, Wisconsin lawyer Carter says the EU follows a stricter approach to intellectual property rules than U.S. law does.

For instance, relatively stringent European restrictions on data collection intended to preserve consumers' privacy apply both to Internet sellers and onsite European retail operations, notes Carter.

These tougher rules can benefit some companies, adds Carter. The EU, for example, offers database protection for significant and unique compilations, while the U.S. does not currently consider databases copyrightable.

Learn As You Go

Even for experienced business lawyers in the United States, coming to terms with developing law and regulation coming out of the EU can seem daunting.

"It's like a law school exam,"says Collins of the international law section. "I often feel like the greatest value I add is not my detailed knowledge of the laws in other countries. It's issue-spotting."

When taking on a new client with European ties, competition concerns are "at the top of my list," says Carter, who represents manufacturers and retailers, as well as IP-related businesses.

In general, "You have to look carefully at what is not going to be permissible under the competition policy in the EU," says Carter. "For example, if you have a manufacturing client that wants to distribute its product in Europe, and it's a product that needs sales and service support, you will need a distributor on the ground. And the EU competition policy does limit restricting the territory. There are restrictions on having distribution agreements be exclusive."

One issue that U.S. practitioners may fail to spot is the potential for legal problems in far-flung locations, says Washington, D.C., attorney Marcuss.

If a client is selling components to a manufacturer in another country, the attorneys involved obviously should review applicable laws of the countries in which both the client and manufacturer are located. But it is also important to consider whether other countries' laws may apply if the completed product is shipped elsewhere, Marcuss says.

Depending on the nature of the product being manufactured, there may be restrictions on its import, or it could even be illegal in other countries, Marcuss notes. Examples of products that are likely to cause regulators particular concern include food, pharmaceuticals, anything that could pose a biohazard, and products that could be considered—or could be used to create—weapons for military or terrorist use.

U.S. lawyers representing companies doing business in Europe also must keep in mind that national laws as well EU regulations may still apply to a variety of business conduct, say experienced practitioners.

In the area of labor and employment, for instance, European law generally does not follow the employment-at-will rule that applies widely in the United States, says Collins.

In Europe, she notes, employment law is a matter of public policy, and laws and collective agreements generally set strict standards on matters such as wages, benefits, termination, and severance pay that are commonly negotiated on an individual basis in the United States. Even termination for cause may not be easy to accomplish in European states because of statutory protections for workers, she says. Consequently, standard provisions in U.S. employment contracts aren't likely to succeed where European workers are concerned.

Similarly, Ragusin says, a common mistake made by U.S. lawyers is using form documents based on American law and assuming those principles can be applied elsewhere because choice of law and choice of forum are located in this country.

"There has to be tremendous caution in understanding that the enforcement likely will have to take place overseas," Ragusin says. "And purely U.S.–styled agreements are not going to be enforceable or fully enforceable."

Ragusin also advises, "Spend a lot of time in crafting a document that's enforceable in multiple jurisdictions, but certainly enforceable against your counterpart in Europe." And if "their documents do not do the trick, then you have to spend months or years trying to pull them out of that sinkhole. So money spent up front is money wisely spent."

And finally, say Ragusin and other experienced practitioners, it's important to maintain perspective in handling a matter that involves foreign law and foreign parties. While the American lawyer likely will play a stronger directional role based on a closer understanding of his or her own client and the client's overall goals, local counsel from another country is likely to have superior knowledge about how things are done there.

As a result, says Ragusin, "That directional role needs to be tempered with humility."

IV. Open Borders

Editor's Introduction

Because of its strong economy and its excellent schools and social services, Europe draws immigrants from less fortunate parts of the world, including the former European colonies of Asia and Africa. These newcomers, even the legal ones, are not particularly welcome. For many Europeans, nationality is defined as ethnicity ("France is the country of the French, Germany of the Germans"), so that people from a different ethnic background will continue to be seen as aliens in their adopted lands even after they have become solid, tax-paying citizens. Many never make it that far but remain in a marginal world of pick-up jobs and social assistance.

In "Containing the Flow," prepared for *Canada and the World Backgrounder*, Europe's immigration problem is set forth alongside Europe's need for immigrants to meet labor shortages and counteract a declining birthrate. (By the middle of this century, one in every three Germans will be over 65, causing many to wonder who will be paying for their pensions.) The authors of *Newsweek*'s "Melting Pot" point out that by discouraging normal economic immigration while maintaining generous policies of asylum, the EU nations may have inadvertently catered to the very immigrants who are least able to support themselves, creating more expense and more resentment in the host countries. There is now, they report, a lively controversy over whether ethnic diversity weakens support for Europe's traditionally generous social services, yet such services will be hard to maintain without the contributions of immigrant labor.

Another immigration dilemma is occurring in Italy, where refugees from North Africa attempt to enter Europe from Libya across the Mediterranean. This problem is discussed by Sophie Arie in her article for *The Christian Science Monitor*, "Italy Plays Role of Europe's Immigration Gatekeeper." Because so many of these asylum-seekers use Libya as their site of embarkation, thereby swelling that country's population by about 2 million, President Muammar Qaddafi has expressed an interest in working with the EU on a policy for processing the refugees and controlling the flow through Libya into Europe.

Besides the people who flock to Europe from other parts of the world, there is also migration within the Union itself, and this too has set off alarms. No sooner had 10 new member nations joined the EU than the 15 established members passed laws to keep East European workers from immediately moving west to look for better jobs and better health care. "Migration and EU Enlargement," from the *OECD Observer*, explores some aspects of labor-related migration, suggesting that the popular image of hungry hordes assailing Fortress Europe is somewhat exaggerated.

Lastly, two articles from *JAMC* (the journal of the Canadian Medical Association) investigate the consequences of open borders for health care throughout Europe. In "Immigration Could Strain EU Health Services," Colin Meek reports on the challenge posed by the high rates of infectious disease in the former Soviet bloc, while in "Czech Republic Fears EU Membership Will Lure Doctors," Dinah A. Spritzer exposes an ironic dilemma: The Czech Republic, which has always maintained a high level of health care, can now expect an influx of patients from all over the EU, just when Czech doctors are leaving for better positions in the West.

Containing the Flow

CANADA AND THE WORLD BACKGROUNDER, DECEMBER 2003

In 1992, a European Commission survey found that 20 million people in Central and Eastern Europe wanted to emigrate to Western Europe. And, it's estimated that at least half a million people enter the EU illegally every year. While many believe legal immigration needs to be easier, others say it's important to manage the flow carefully.

Europe is connected to the Middle East and Asia by land, and is within eyesight of Africa across the Straits of Gibraltar. The affluent lifestyle enjoyed by most Europeans is a magnet for the desperately poor people who live on its edges. Many people are prepared to risk everything—including their lives—to get inside the continent's walls. In February 2003, for example, 18 migrants set out from sub-Saharan Africa and headed for the Canary Islands, Spanish territory in the Atlantic Ocean. But, 12 of them died on the way and the others survived by gnawing the wood of their boat for moisture. The migrants paid the equivalent of $800 each to board the small, open fishing boat, which they thought was their ticket to a better life, a journey that thousands of Africans make every year. Their dreams might have come true had the boat's motor not failed: then, the two "captains" were picked up by another boat, but the migrants were left to fend for themselves on a stormy sea.

Keeping Europe from being swamped by economic migrants is a major challenge that's only going to grow bigger. These migrants are joined by people facing persecution in their native lands because of their race, political beliefs, or religious faith. They are attracted by Europe's freedoms of speech, association, and worship.

Immigration is a hotly debated issue in Europe, which faces huge labour shortages over the next decades, especially in high-tech sectors. The United Nations has predicted that an aging Europe will need about 160 million immigrants to meet its labour needs over the next 25 years. And, many governments have recognized they will not be able to fund their pension systems without large-scale immigration over the next two to three decades. In Italy, for example, there were eight workers to every pensioner in the 1950s, compared to fewer than four by 2000: without immigration, it's estimated that number will drop to 1.5 by 2050. While the European Commission, the EU's executive body, proposed new rules (in 2001) to co-ordinate immigration policy across the continent, making it easier for foreigners to find work in the 15 member states, it was felt that making legal immigration easier should go hand in hand with harsher penalties for people smugglers.

The would-be settlers are running into a lot of hostility from European residents; far-right, anti-immigrant political parties are picking up support in surprising places such as usually tolerant Holland and Denmark. By 2002, a pattern was emerging across the continent with centre-left and social democratic governments losing power to centre-right governments. Political parties that campaigned against immigration were gaining popularity. The left had lost power in Austria, Italy, Denmark, Portugal, and the Netherlands. In France, the Socialists' candidate didn't reach the final round of the presidential election, knocked out by an extreme right-wing candidate (Jean-Marie Le Pen). He was described by the *Economist* as "a populist thug . . . (bearing) the ugly face of extreme nationalism (who) spreads hatred."

John Lloyd, a London-based journalist and former editor of the *New Statesman*, says extremist immigrant groups have left many

---

Immigration controls remain, and "the popular voices opposing large-scale immigration swell."—John Lloyd, a London-based journalist

---

Europeans feeling vulnerable. "The spectacle of men claiming to be seeking sanctuary from persecution being arrested for, or charged with, crimes that seem to foreshadow murder, even mass murder, has made a deep impression," he writes in the *Globe and Mail* in January 2003. But he says the more extreme political parties are losing some ground. He cites the general election in the Netherlands in January 2003, where "(an anti-immigration) party named after its murdered leader—Pim Fortuyn's List—saw its support cut by two-thirds. It had, last year, come second after the conservative Christian Democrats, beating the Labour Party into third place. Now, these two parties again dominate the scene, with the conservatives slightly ahead."

Nevertheless, he says the immigration controls remain, and "the popular voices opposing large-scale immigration swell."

He says that even a left-wing economics professor at Cambridge University (Professor Bob Rowthorn) has some reservations about too much immigration. The problem, says Professor Rowthorn, "is that the potential flow of migrants is so great. Without barriers . . . there would be a massive and unacceptable flow of migrants into rich countries."

In an article in the February 2003 issue of *Prospect* magazine (a political and cultural magazine published in London, England), Professor Rowthorn wrote: "Immigration on a modest scale brings benefits in the form of diversity and new ideas, but the pace of the present transformation in Europe worries me. I believe it is a recipe for conflict."

He says that, while there are no official statistics on the ethnicity of migrants, data on their geographical origin "suggest that, over the past three years, the net immigration of people from ethnic minorities has averaged about 100,000 per annum. With immigration on this scale, the ethnic minority population, including people of mixed race, could reach 20 percent of the population by 2050."

The answer, he says, is not to open the doors to immigrants but to raise the standard of living in countries around the world so people don't want to leave them. John Lloyd says the only problem with that prospect is that it's a century away from becoming a reality.

Melting Pot

By Stryker McGuire, et al.
Newsweek, May 3, 2004

Imigracja. Indvandring. Inmigracioón. By whatever name, immigration is on Europe's mind these days. To the typical man on the street of old Europe, enlargement means more workers moving across more borders to take more jobs—legally. The accession of 10 new members on May 1 also means new, often porous borders for job seekers arriving from outside the EU—illegally. This isn't necessarily bad news, from an economic standpoint. But no matter how many studies attest to the theoretical benefits of immigration, the natives still get restless—and so do politicians.

In this climate of unease, a fierce debate has surfaced in Britain and drawn attention across Europe. It emerged not from the political right, where most immigration issues erupt, but from the left, where European progressives are pondering a troubling new dilemma: will mass immigration be the undoing of Europe's cherished welfare state?

The argument goes like this: immigration brings diversity, which erodes the sense of shared values and solidarity that has kept enlightened European socialism alive in a world of free markets and rampant capitalism. Those debating the point talk of models. They look at Sweden and see a fairly homogenous society of taxpayers happy to fork over 60 percent of their income in exchange for generous social benefits. They look at America and see a wildly diverse society whose taxes—under 30 percent, on average—provide for only the flimsiest of safety nets. No national health insurance, no long-term unemployment benefits, no security of the sort that Western Europeans take for granted. As immigration, legal and illegal, begins to transform much of Europe into a melting pot, they realize they may soon face a set of seemingly impossible choices. Will their Europe of the future remain like Sweden, or become more like America? And is there a trade-off between solidarity and diversity, such that Europe's social-welfare states can survive?

The choice may not be quite that stark. But clearly, immigration will reshape Europe. Its population is aging rapidly, dragging down economic growth and putting tremendous pressure on underfunded pensions. According to the American demographer Bill Frey, the median age in the EU by 2050 will be 52.7 years, compared with 36.2 years in the United States.

Enlargement will do little to ease Europe's demographic bind. Birth rates in Estonia, Lithuania, and the Czech Republic are among the lowest in the world. Immigration from outside the new 25-member EU will therefore become essential to Europe's economic well-being. But that very fact will force adjustments. Europe's sizable non-Christian minority is already the fastest-growing segment of the continental population, and in some countries that has become a source of deep anxiety. The Netherlands, by some estimates, will have a school-age Muslim majority by 2050.

Such trends cannot help but have a major impact on social policy. Unlike the United States, where large-scale (but relatively well-managed) immigration has helped boost American productivity and entrepreneurship, Europe has largely discouraged economic immigration. The result: migrants from around the world found the only way to live and work in Europe was, in effect, to break in and claim asylum. "You're left with a situation in which every immigrant begins to look problematic," says Charles Westin of Stockholm University. Ferruccio Pastore of the Center for the Study of International Politics in Rome says the system suffers from "chronic immigration schizophrenia."

Immigration from outside the new 25-member EU will . . . become essential to Europe's economic well-being.

One consequence has been to rob Europe of much of the beneficial effects of foreign labor. Through the early 1990s, Germany had no comprehensive immigration policy. It did have one of the world's most liberal asylum laws, and attracted more than 1 million refugees during just a few years. The laws have since changed and the numbers declined, but immigrants remain disproportionately dependent on state assistance: 8.3 percent of immigrants are on welfare, compared with 3.3 percent of native Germans. Similarly, joblessness among immigrants (21.2 percent) is more than twice that of the German-born population. "For 50 years," says Stephanie Wahl of the Institute for Economics and Society in Bonn, "we've taken in poorly skilled immigrants without thinking much about what would happen."

The picture was much the same across the rest of Europe. And politicians reacted in much the same way. Rather than tackle difficult underlying economic issues, they went after "asylum seekers"—Europe's catchall phrase for virtually all immigrants—urged on by baying tabloids and insecure citizenries. From Dublin to Berlin, governments cracked down. Germany began turning away refugees. It sped up deportation procedures and cut welfare payments. Asylum applications are now down to about 50,000 a year.

This climate of fear still rules. In advance of the May 1 enlargement, alarmed by the prospect of invading East European job seekers, Denmark's conservative government passed a law granting benefits to immigrants only after they've been in the country for seven years. Germany's socialists, along with most other EU governments, adopted similar measures. The barriers take different forms, from residency tests and waiting periods to outright prohibitions. But these are little more than stopgaps. With time, more-enlightened measures will surely be adopted. Britain, France, Germany, and Spain, in fact, are moving toward U.S.–style policies. By managing and controlling immigration, they hope to reap the economic benefits of immigration while muting public unease.

But will it work? This is the unsettling question posed recently by David Goodhart, a respected voice of the British left who started thinking about immigration and its effect on the traditional welfare state that sits at the core of Europe's identity. In a 6,200-word article titled "Too Diverse?" in the February issue of *Prospect*, the current-affairs magazine he edits, Goodhart sparked a great row by suggesting that diversity and social welfare don't mix. His thesis: Europe's welfare state thrives on homogeneity. People who are alike find it easier to give up something (e.g., taxes) to take care of one another. Diversity, he argues, might undermine this social compact, as it has in America. "To put it bluntly," he wrote, "most of us prefer our own kind." We share our wealth when "people like us" fall into hardship and need help; we are wary of immigrants or others who might not share those values, partly for fear that they will exploit the system and our generosity.

Goodhart, though deliberately provocative, still did not foresee the firestorm that greeted his article—especially after it was reprinted in the *Guardian* newspaper for a wider audience. In response, A. Sivanandan of the Institute of Race Relations likened the essay to Thatcherite Little Englandism dressed up "in liberal rhetoric and pseudo-intellectualism." the *Guardian*'s Gary Younge wrote: "There is indeed a progressive dilemma. It's the dilemma of what to do with people who pose as progressives and preach like reactionaries."

For a change, however, the debate over immigration was liberated from London's tabloids and entered the intellectual and political mainstream. Whether Goodhart is right or not is almost moot. "All the survey evidence indicates that as society becomes more diverse, support for public spending on core state services increases," writes Peter Taylor-Gooby of the University of Kent. Or maybe not, suggests Peter Lindert, author of "Social Spending and Economic Growth Since the 18th Century." Immigration, he says, "lowers society's willingness to tax and spend on social services"—but it shouldn't, he says. "The political tensions are based on a false premise." The fact is, Europe's future is a huge and irreversible social experiment. Europe needs to get it right.

Italy Plays Role of Europe's Immigration Gatekeeper

BY SOPHIE ARIE
THE CHRISTIAN SCIENCE MONITOR, SEPTEMBER 9, 2004

When a 9-year-old Somali girl named Asma arrived on the Italian island of Lampedusa in a rickety boat full of illegal immigrants earlier this year, she was in shock. She and her parents had watched helplessly as three of her siblings died during the dangerous journey across the Mediterranean from Libya.

This summer, Italy has once again been horrified as boatloads of exhausted refugees limp into its ports, having set out, mostly from the coast of Libya in North Africa, hoping to sneak into Europe.

Italy, which struggles to patrol its 1,500 miles of porous coastline, is battling to dispel its image as an easy entry point onto the Continent. And it is calling on the European Union for help. After all, once immigrants penetrate Italy or Spain by sea from North Africa, the new arrivals are free to spread through 15 other European countries whose shared borders are open under the Schengen border agreement.

"Effectively the Italians and the Spanish are patrolling not just their own, but Europe's, borders. So the Italians say Europe should play a bigger part in solving the problem," says Sergio Romano, a political commentator and former Italian ambassador to Russia.

Italy wants Europe to draw up a common immigration policy, creating joint European border patrols, immigrant quotas, and strict asylum guidelines. But with immigration an increasingly politicized issue across Europe, individual countries are unlikely to reach rapid consensus.

Last month, Italy and Germany raised the idea of opening "reception centers" inside Libya to process asylum requests and fly failed asylum seekers back to their country of origin—other African and Middle Eastern nations. European lawmakers and human rights advocates have balked at the concept, warning that it would create "concentration camps" in the desert of North Africa.

Italian lawmaker Rocco Buttiglione, who will be in charge of EU policy on asylum and immigration once he is sworn in as justice commissioner next month, insists that the centers would help people find legal ways into Europe and avoid falling into the hands of criminals smuggling people.

EU figures estimate around 500,000 illegal immigrants arrive in Europe each year from all over the world. The Italian Interior Ministry estimates that immigration into Europe is worth more than $3 billion per year, the trip across the Mediterranean alone costing as much as 2,000 euros ($2,400) per person.

Libya has yet to comment on the proposed camps, but President Muammar Qaddafi has been eager to engage Europe on the issue. This autumn the EU is expected to discuss lifting its embargo on Libya, put in place because of the country's past ties to terrorism. Of late Mr. Qaddafi has tried to build bridges to the West after decades of isolation.

"Qaddafi will try to use this situation to undo the damage done by embargoes over the years," says Mr. Romano.

Italian Prime Minister Silvio Berlusconi traveled to Libya last month to discuss immigration with Qaddafi. Mr. Berlusconi called the talks "meaningful" and said the two leaders were facing "a problem that isn't just Italian and Libyan, but European and African."

Libya has reportedly already begun to police its borders with Chad, Niger, and Sudan, ultimately to start pushing the immigration front line further south into Africa.

"If for you Italians illegal immigration is a problem, for us it's much more—it's an invasion," Libyan foreign minister Mohammed Abdel-Rahman Shalgham told *La Stampa*, an Italian newspaper, in an interview.

Libya is negotiating with the EU for more financial and technological assistance, such as radars, night-vision equipment, bullet-proof patrol boats, and aircraft.

On its own, Italy has managed to significantly reduce illegal immigration by strengthening its coastal patrols. The flow of illegal immigrants to Italy dropped by 40 percent, from 23,719 in 2002 to 14,331 in 2003, according to government figures. This year, the number of boats arriving has fallen by another 25 percent.

The decline, however, is mostly from a reduction in immigration from Eastern Europe. Libya, according to Italy's Interior Minister Giuseppe Pisanu, has become a kind of immigrant bottleneck, with up to 2 million would-be immigrants from all over Africa and the Middle East currently waiting there for a place on a boat to Europe.

Asma is only one of many bedraggled *clandestini* who have told of horrific conditions in the desert outside Tripoli. She described being locked in a shed with her family for days as jeeploads of people from different countries continued to arrive.

"They kept us all in there, without letting us out, scolding anyone who asked any questions," Asma told journalists in Lampedusa. "We stayed there for four days. Other people were even there for 20 days or more."

Migration and EU Enlargement

OECD OBSERVER, MAY 2004

One of the great dreams of European integration since the Treaty of Rome has been to create a completely unified labour market, though this has proven hard to achieve in reality. Even among the present EU 15, while free movement of persons and labour market access for workers is possible, obstacles continue to exist, like recognition of qualifications and access to social welfare benefits.

In addition, there are obvious language barriers which slow down mobility, as well as the reduction of wage differentials between immigrants and nationals. In most cases, workers from Poland or Hungary or any of the other new members will not be free to seek work in another EU country under normal conditions for several years. This is because a majority of member states have introduced transition periods ranging from two to seven years, in order to stem a possible increased inflow of new migrants from eastern Europe and the pressures this would entail. Some countries, such as Ireland, Sweden, and the United Kingdom, will not be imposing transitional arrangements, while the Netherlands and Portugal will impose a quota. Is their prudence worth it? Would immigration from new accession members suddenly rise if a transition phase were not introduced?

Not necessarily. In the past, immigrants into European countries, except for Germany and Austria, came predominantly from countries outside Europe, from Asia and North Africa, for instance. Flows from eastern Europe also concern non-European OECD countries, for example, Poles and Hungarians to the United States, Canada, and Australia. For historical reasons, countries have received immigrants of different origins. Moroccans and Algerians are common in France, Turks and former Yugoslavians in Germany and the Netherlands, and Pakistanis and Indians in the UK, to cite some well-known examples. During other periods of EU enlargement to include Greece (1981), and Spain and Portugal (1986), migration did not rise. In the case of Spain, return migration had occurred before accession. The bulk of immigration from southern Europe occurred mainly and massively during the 1950s and 1960s. These migrants built communities that then acted as a draw on new immigrants. The links between EU accession countries and existing EU member states are probably more diffuse.

OECD Directorate for Employment, Labour and Social Affairs (2004), "Migration and EU Enlargement," *The OECD Observer*, No. 243, OECD, Paris, pp. 28–29.

Flows from the east might grow in importance, but probably not from the accession countries; other countries such as Romania, Moldavia, and the Ukraine may be more important sources.

The renewed interest in labour-related migration in many OECD countries in the last decade, as well as the predominance of family reunification and the great number of asylum seekers, counters criticism of what is termed "Fortress Europe." The number of immigrants, including from outside the EU, has risen far more sharply in Europe over the last decade than in the United States.

One reason for policy prudence towards foreign workers is that immigration can raise social costs, in education and healthcare, for instance. But can migrants alleviate these costs, too? The immediate costs are in healthcare and social protection, especially for humanitarian immigration. Educational costs are high also, especially in cases of accompanying dependents or family reunification.

One of the most hotly debated questions is whether a large increase in immigration flows would help OECD countries pay for their future social spending, especially on pensions. The argument is that more young immigrants mean more young workers and so more revenue for social services and pension funds. In this hypothesis, the focus is mainly on employing high-skilled immigrants who will come for a temporary period rather than on recruiting more low-skilled workers. However, this thinking has its flaws. The most obvious is that immigrants are frequently not temporary and may wish to settle and retire in the host country themselves. And their population is ageing too, to become tomorrow's pensioners. Furthermore, not all legal immigrants join the workforce. In Australia and Canada, countries which operate selective immigration policies based on labour market needs, only a quarter to a third of annual entrants are active workers, the rest being family dependents, including school-age children.

Another limit is whether the immigrants actually find work. The unemployment rate among foreigners in some European OECD countries is twice that of their percentage in the total labour force. Those who do find work are often paid less than native workers. Indeed, some OECD countries have begun focusing more energy and finance on training and supporting new arrivals, in part to help them to integrate more rapidly into the labour market or to retain those who might otherwise move on to competitor countries. But while such policies can help integrate foreign populations and overcome certain labour shortages, immigration alone cannot generate sufficient funds required to finance the increasing demands of ageing populations.

Immigration Could Strain EU Health Services

By Colin Meek
Canadian Medical Association Journal, August 3, 2004

Physicians and politicians are warning that the new European Union membership of former East Bloc countries with high rates of infectious diseases could strain the continent's public health resources.

In May, 10 countries, many of them former Communist states, joined the EU, sparking an intense debate over the prospect of increased demand for health services across the continent.

Under the EU's Charter of Fundamental Rights, adopted in 2002, all patients have the right to treatment in any member state. A series of European Court of Justice rulings have also confirmed that patients having trouble receiving care in their home country may seek treatment in another EU state. Their home government is required to reimburse the costs.

As of June 1, a new European health insurance card also made it easier for EU citizens to access care while they are travelling or working temporarily in another EU country.

These rights mean patients may seek treatment outside their country's borders.

Improving the health status of former Soviet bloc countries will be a "major challenge," warned David Byrne, the European commissioner for health and consumer protection.

"With EU enlargement, our borders will shift to the East," Byrne said. "Russia, Ukraine, Belarus, and others will soon be on our doorstep and will require even greater attention. We need to persuade our partners that preventing HIV/AIDS is just as vital to their future economic well-being as roads or power stations."

Doctors from the European Centre on Health Societies in Transition and the Imperial College London joined the warning chorus in April (*Lancet* 2004; 363:1389–92), stating that "public health systems, rooted in Soviet traditions, are struggling to respond effectively" to diseases such as tuberculosis and HIV.

Epidemics have been reported in Russia, Ukraine, and Belarus—countries that now border the EU. In the paper, the doctors say movement within the EU raises questions about the possible spread of those diseases.

In Western Europe, widespread concern has centred around the prospect of this potential surge in immigration. In the UK, the lobby group Immigration Watch claims between 40,000 and 50,000 workers will move to the UK from the East each year, in part because of better quality health care. Official predictions put the likely immigration rate closer to 10,000 per year.

In Eastern Europe, medical associations are worried higher wages in the West will prompt the mass emigration of doctors [see the following article on the Czech Republic].

Aware of the widespread confusion around patients' rights that these debates have stimulated, the EU Commission has established a high-level group of senior health officials from the member states to improve cooperation around the issue.

Czech Republic Fears EU Membership Will Lure Doctors

By Dinah A. Spritzer
Canadian Medical Association Journal, August 3, 2004

The Czech Republic's health insurance system is braced for an onslaught of new claims following the Eastern European country's entrance into the European Union in May.

Generally regarded as practising the highest standard of medical care in the former Eastern bloc, the Czech Republic is expected to be a mecca for patients from EU countries seeking better quality treatment than they can get at home.

"Middle class Russians or Arabs who want good care but can't afford the Mayo Clinic might . . . [already] come to the Czech Republic," says Pavel Hrobon, a Czech physician and health administrator.

In addition, there will be a shift in the physician workforce. Czech doctors earn about 35,000 crowns a month (Can$1785)—a quarter of the average income for physicians in neighbouring Germany. Hrobon predicts that 5% of doctors will seek work elsewhere. But David Rath, head of the Czech Chamber of Doctors, estimates the exodus will reach 30%.

Dr. Pavel Machac, an anesthesiologist at Prague's Nemocnice Hospital, says he is among those who will head West. "Here you are forced to work massive overtime even though it is against EU rules," says Machac. "I want to be in a country where I am treated more fairly."

Some specialists do work excessive hours due to an uneven distribution throughout the Republic.

Health Minister Jozef Kubinyi has attempted to quash fears of both a doctor shortage and an influx of patients. He points to the offsetting arrival of Slovak and Polish doctors who get paid more in the Czech Republic.

Patients will only be motivated to come to the Czech Republic for elective procedures, such as dentistry and plastic surgery, that they have to pay for out-of-pocket, he says.

The vast majority of Czech citizens are covered by the nine public insurance companies. Private insurers supplement what is offered.

"News: Czech Republic Fears EU Membership Will Lure Doctors"—Reprinted from *CMAJ* 03-Aug-04; 171(3), Pages 224–225 by permission of the publisher. © 2004 Canadian Medical Association.

If patients do arrive from other Eastern bloc countries seeking Western-style medicine, they will also find a country with almost no waiting times for operations. There are only 330 people per doctor in the Czech Republic, compared to 650 people per doctor in Great Britain.

The country's nine public health care insurers are the entity most likely to be affected by the country's entrance into the EU, since the families of workers from EU countries will now qualify for benefits, even if they are non-residents. Visitors requiring emergency care will also be covered. In addition, the government anticipates an influx of pensioners from Western Europe because of the Czech Republic's lower cost of living.

Ladilslav Svec, director of the Prague-based Center for International Reimbursements, said insurers will have to spend time and money "evaluating the concrete situation of concrete individuals," to determine if they meet residency requirements that entitle them to benefits.

Perhaps the most pressing problem, Svec says, is the 70,000 Slovaks working in the Czech Republic who will now be covered by Czech insurance companies. Those returning to live in Slovakia, also now an EU member, are entitled to Czech health coverage even after they permanently leave the Czech Republic.

Insurance companies are already infamous in the Czech Republic for not paying doctors on time, so some critics question whether they will have trouble reimbursing foreign hospitals when Czechs get ill while they are abroad.

"It's estimated that international clearing of payments between insurance companies in the enlarged EU will take an average of three years," says Hrobon.

The Czech healthcare sector is running a deficit of 10 billion crowns (Cdn$52 million) and co-payments, as well as a closing of numerous hospitals, may be a necessity.

In such a bankrupt system, foreigners can expect to find well-educated doctors, but preventive care and even toilet paper are not always options.

V. EU Security and Relations with the U.S.

Editor's Introduction

Questions of security seem to have become increasingly urgent everywhere, and Europe is no exception. The opening of borders within the EU may have created new opportunities for criminals and terrorists, since the various police and national security forces have been slow to coordinate actions and jealous about sharing information. However, in January 2004 the EU established a pan-European arrest warrant, and July saw the well-publicized capture of a French serial killer who had long avoided detection by living in Belgium, where the authorities were unaware of his record. This coup was only mildly reassuring to the European-in-the-street, however; many people feel that the Union should be moving faster to integrate security and intelligence services, especially after the Madrid train bombings of March 2004 and Al Qaeda's subsequent threats against nations that had joined the U.S.–led war in Iraq. Honor Mahony's "Commission Proposes Crisis Centre for Terrorist Attacks" from *EUobserver* provides an account of plans to coordinate the response to any future terrorist attack.

The Madrid attack was the most deadly terrorist action ever carried out in Europe, but it was not the first. A number of European countries—notably, France, Germany, Great Britain, Italy, and Spain—have had extensive experience with terrorist groups at home; some have also faced popular uprisings abroad. In "Military Skills Key to European Influence in U.S." from the *Washington Times*, Louis R. Golino reviews a think-tank report about the strengths and weaknesses of Europe's military forces and suggests that the EU's collective experience with urban terrorism and insurgency may constitute a unique asset, making the Union a valued ally of the more powerful United States in wartime.

At present only a few European countries have a substantial military, and the European Union's own forces are small. Ever since World War II, the United States has been the primary defender of Europe through the North Atlantic Treaty Organization (NATO), which was originally intended to protect Western Europe from a possible Soviet invasion. (The Soviet-controlled countries of Eastern Europe had a similar organization called the Warsaw Pact, but this dissolved when the Soviet Union collapsed in 1989, whereupon most of the Eastern European countries applied to join NATO too.) With the end of the Cold War, the Soviet threat has practically vanished, leaving the future of NATO in doubt. Although it is still Europe's dominant military alliance, it may have outlived its mission. Many Americans would like to see the European countries shoulder the burden of their own defense, and the EU does seem to offer a collective base for that. In December 2004, a newly organized EU force took over NATO's nine-year-old peacekeeping mission in Bosnia, in the Union's most extensive military endeavor yet. However, the United

States is not entirely happy about the prospect of a thoroughly independent Europe with armies of its own, nor does that seem a likely development in the immediate future—there are too many problems of financing and organization. In the long run, though, Europe's military and diplomatic relations with the United States may be redefined through the EU, outside of NATO, as Andrew Moravcsik predicts in "Europe Takes Charge" from *Newsweek*.

Meanwhile, the invasion of Iraq has split the Union into pro- and anti-American camps, with Britain and most of the East European nations supporting the United States, while France and Germany warn against the dangers of letting America lead Europe into war. In "EU 'Must Work with U.S. As an Ally,'" Toby Helm reports the views of Tony Blair, the British prime minister, who has committed troops to the war and who generally feels that cooperation with the United States is a must for Europe's future. Ironically, as Sam Natapoff points out in "A More Perfect Union?" Blair was the first British prime minister to openly favor the Union and work for its goals; now he is at the center of a deep split that affects the proposed new constitution and the integration of new members, as well as Britain's future in the EU and the EU's future in world affairs.

Finally, in "Transatlantic Divides," Wen Stephenson of the *Boston Globe* interviews British author Timothy Garton Ash, who discusses the relationship of EU nations—both individually and as a single body—with the United States. Garton Ash reflects on how British support of the United States in the Iraq War has driven a wedge between Great Britain and several EU members, and he concludes that the "future of freedom" in the world depends on the EU and America resolving their differences.

Commission Proposes Crisis Centre for Terrorist Attacks

By Honor Mahony
EUobserver, October 21, 2004

The European Commission has proposed setting up an emergency crisis centre to deal specifically with terrorist attacks in the European Union.

This centre would "bring together representatives of all relevant Commission services during an emergency," says the proposal—one of a series of anti-terrorism measures published by the Commission on Wednesday (20 October).

It is also proposed that a general rapid alert system, to be named after the multi-eyed Greek God Argus, be set up to link all of the specialised emergencies systems that can be found in the various member states.

"Certain emergency situations may be of such gravity . . . that overall coordination across virtually all EU policies is necessary," says the paper.

The Brussels executive also recommends that at least 1 billion euro a year is spent on research on security in the EU.

Energy, communications, health, food, and transport are among those "critical infrastructures" that are at increased risk of "catastrophic terrorist attacks."

Madrid Attacks

Referring specifically to the biggest terrorist attack on European soil, the Madrid attack in March, the paper says that support to the victims and families of terrorist attacks must be "an integral part of the response."

"The Commission intends to contribute to honouring the memories of the victims of the 11 March 2004 outrage, through the ceremonies to be held on the 1st European day of the victims of terrorism, on 11 March 2005."

That date is also to become a general day for having "civic and democratic" debates on securing freedom.

Charities

On the financing of terrorism, the Brussels executive suggests stepping up its scrutiny of charities—an area where it is thought a substantial chunk of the money that eventually ends up in terrorists hands' is channelled.

"Many such organisations raise money destined for conflict zones. Once money arrives in such areas, the ability to rely on international co-operation, in order to trace its destination, is much reduced," says the paper.

Where Does This All Fit In?

The proposals—four separate communications by the European Commission—will be presented on Monday to EU justice ministers.

However, the Council and the EU's anti-terrorism co-ordinator Gijs de Vries also have to propose measures—which will eventually go to EU leaders for approval.

If and when such proposals see the light of day is up to member states.

"It's up to them to say whether it's a first priority," said a Commission official on Wednesday.

Military Skills Key to European Influence in U.S.

By Louis R. Golino
The Washington Times, July 18, 2004

A new report from a British think tank says that to enhance their influence in Washington and the world, European governments need to improve their military capabilities and develop their own distinctive approach to warfare.

That approach should build on core European military strengths related to postwar stabilization after a military conflict. These approaches include nation-building, peacekeeping, and counter-insurgency warfare.

The United States also has much to learn from its European allies about these approaches, the report said, especially as both Europe and the United States work to stabilize, rebuild, and establish democratic regimes in Iraq and Afghanistan. Moreover, the report suggests that Britain and France, Europe's leading military powers, lead by example in developing a European way of war and a common European approach to relations with the United States, based on partnership and autonomy.

The report highlights the need for Europeans to retain the ability to work alongside U.S. military forces, which are becoming increasingly sophisticated technologically, because Europeans are not expected to undertake major military operations at the higher end of the conflict spectrum without the United States.

The report further suggests that Europe develop military forces that complement those of the United States and reflect the changing nature of warfare. Toward that end, it says Europeans need better combat skills and equipment.

It also recommends that the United States enhance capabilities related to the post-conflict period, or winning the peace, specifically by increasing the number of troops that are trained for peacekeeping and nation-building. European forces have more extensive experience than American forces in those tasks as a result of European colonialism and their recent nation-building efforts in the Balkans and elsewhere.

EU Military Operations

Last year, the European Union mounted its first military operations by working with NATO to enforce the peace in Macedonia, leading police missions in Bosnia and Macedonia, and undertaking its first independent, long-range military deployment, which was in the Congo. At the end of this year, the EU will take over command of a large peacekeeping mission in Bosnia from NATO through an arrangement known as Berlin Plus, under which the EU can use NATO military assets. NATO, however, will retain a presence in this region after the handover.

NATO leaders agreed at a summit in Istanbul last month to train Iraqi security forces and to expand the alliance's peacekeeping force in Afghanistan. EU leaders agreed on a constitutional treaty last month that aims, among other goals, to enhance the bloc's global profile by creating an EU president and foreign minister. They also agreed to create an EU diplomatic corps and an EU defense agency that will work to strengthen European military capabilities with better procurement decisions and increased resources for military research and development.

Moreover, EU leaders appointed Portuguese prime minister José Manuel Barroso as the next president of the European Commission and reappointed Javier Solana as EU foreign policy chief. Solana is expected to become the first foreign minister of the EU.

A European Way of War, published by the Center for European Reform (CER), a London-based research institute that focuses on European integration, was prepared by six prominent defense analysts from both sides of the Atlantic. They include Michael O'Hanlon, an American defense expert at the Brookings Institution, and five Europeans. The Europeans include Charles Grant, director of the CER; Steven Everts, director of the CER's transatlantic program; and Daniel Keohane, a fellow at the CER.

The other European authors are Lawrence Freedman, one of Britain's best-known authorities on defense policy and a professor of war studies at King's College of Oxford University, and François Heisbourg, a prominent French defense expert who is director of the Paris-based Foundation for Strategic Research and chairman of the International Institute for Strategic Studies in London.

America as Benchmark

These authors explain that U.S. military forces are widely viewed as the inevitable benchmark for assessing Europe's progress in enhancing its military power. For example, military experts often note that Europeans collectively spend about two-thirds as much as the United States on defense but have only about one-tenth of the U.S. capacity for force projection and only half of the latter forces can be deployed rapidly.

Such comparisons unfairly slight European military contributions, these experts said, because Europe has different strategic priorities from the United States and does not need, nor could it afford, to emulate the overwhelming U.S. military prowess.

The authors said that vast increases in defense spending, which in any case would be extremely unpopular among European citizens, are not necessary to enhance European military capabilities because the required capabilities can be developed by using existing funds more efficiently and by better allocating current resources instead of directing the bulk of them toward maintaining conscript armies.

Defense experts say that in addition to certain key capabilities that are lacking, such as improved communications and logistics, Europe needs additional professional military forces. Grant added that in some issues, such as air-to-ground cruise missiles and air-to-air missiles, European equipment is superior to that of the United States.

> *Defense experts say that . . . Europe needs additional professional military forces.*

The British Model

The British military provides a more suitable model for continental European militaries than does the U.S. military, said Freedman of Oxford. The British model, he said, is based primarily on the importance of separating insurgents from local populations and working closely with the locals.

Freedman called U.S. military doctrine "dysfunctional" because of the reluctance of U.S. military commanders to engage in the unconventional warfare associated with counterinsurgency and peace enforcement operations. U.S. concern about force protection, he said, "often leads to overreaction by [American] soldiers that pushes insurgents and locals together."

In recent months, British military commanders in Iraq reportedly have said that their American counterparts have used overly aggressive tactics against insurgents in Iraq, especially in Fallujah, which they say has heightened Iraqi concerns about the U.S. military presence.

Freedman also suggested that a new war sequence has emerged as a result of Iraq and other recent conflicts, in which actual warfighting ends relatively quickly because no enemy can match U.S. military power, but the postconflict period can become almost indefinite. As a result, he added: "The key question is not whether the Europeans can adapt to American military doctrine but whether the Americans can adapt to the European way of war."

Division of Labor

According to the conventional wisdom among defense experts, O'Hanlon of the Brookings Institution explained, there is a division of labor in trans-Atlantic military operations in which the U.S. "cooks dinner" while Europeans "do the dishes." That analogy is a reference to how the United States dominates military campaigns because of its overwhelming military forces, but Europeans are often left to carry the largest peacekeeping burden because of their strengths in that task. As O'Hanlon said, "European soldiers are arguably better at peacekeeping than U.S. forces."

He rejected the notion that there is or should be a neat trans-Atlantic military division of labor, however, explaining that each side of the Atlantic needs both combat and peace enforcement capabilities.

O'Hanlon also said the distinction between the combat and post-combat phases of military conflict is eroding because postconflict stabilization can require high-intensity combat operations, as happened recently in Iraq. As he said: "Iraq has demonstrated that the U.S. needs to be good—and indeed get better—at postconflict stabilization."

He also suggested that European militaries use Britain as a model by developing "somewhat smaller professional forces that are well-provisioned logistically, even on a remote battlefield."

U.S. Concerns

Ever since the EU began the drive to develop its own military forces in 1999, U.S. officials and commentators have raised two main concerns: that an independent European military might become a competitor to NATO and that the Europeans would duplicate what was done through NATO to enhance their military capabilities.

As Everts and Keohane explained in *A European Way of War*, however, such concerns are largely misplaced: "The reality is the EU will not have its own army for decades to come—if ever, nor will NATO's status as Europe's preeminent defense organization change any time soon.

"For most European defense ministries," they wrote, "NATO will continue to be the principal multinational military organization. That is not only because NATO is a military organization—which the EU is not—but also because of NATO's large and experienced military headquarters."

They also pointed out that NATO, rather than the EU, is currently providing the main impetus for reform of European military forces—primarily through the NATO Response Force and the NATO command in Norfolk—that promote trans-Atlantic military transformation.

European countries are developing military forces designed to enable them to keep up with the U.S. "revolution in military affairs," which uses digital technology to improve the battlefield assessments of military commanders. Moreover, EU officials frequently explain that European military forces are available for both NATO and EU missions and are intended for use when the United States decides not to participate. Most European countries belong to both organizations.

EU vs. NATO

In the past couple of decades, EU integration was dominated by efforts to create the euro and establish a single market, said Charles Grant, the CER director. "In the coming decades, it will be cooperation on justice and home affairs, and also on foreign and defense policy, that drives European integration."

"Justice and home affairs" refers to police and judicial coopera-

---

Unlike NATO and other international organizations, the EU can draw on a unique combination of hard and soft power.

---

tion and efforts to protect the EU's homeland security. EU countries have stepped up their efforts in those tasks since the March 11 terrorist attacks in Madrid, such as by appointing a terrorism policy czar, although they still have a long way to go to develop an effective antiterrorism strategy, according to the CER report.

Grant also discussed the differences between the EU and NATO, noting that, unlike NATO and other international organizations, the EU can draw on a unique combination of hard and soft power, or on "the military and civilian instruments for managing crises." As he explained, the lesson of recent interventions in Afghanistan and Iraq is that hard power is sufficient to overthrow a regime, but stabilizing and rebuilding a country requires the use of soft power. Moreover, the main strengths of the EU, which until recently has been a civilian power, lie in the domain of soft power.

Grant also said that, although Europeans are criticized for being overly bureaucratic and for emphasizing institutions over capabilities, the NATO bureaucracy is substantially larger than the nascent EU military bureaucracy. NATO has a headquarters staff in Brussels of almost 20,000, but the embryonic EU defense agency has fewer than 300 staff.

Relations with Washington

The CER report concludes that the key issue in the European defense policy debate is what relationship to pursue with Washington. As Freedman of Oxford explained, Europe has two main approaches to relations with the U.S.—the French and British perspectives: France believes that Europe should enhance its ability to act independently in the military realm to build Europe as a counterweight to the United States. Britain, in contrast, said Freedman, believes that by enhancing its military capabilities and pursuing a partnership with the United States, Europe stands a better chance of Washington's taking its views into account.

As Grant has argued elsewhere, the French are too quick to oppose the United States, but the British tend to support the United States reflexively. Moreover, as the report's authors noted, these internal European divisions substantially reduced European influence on recent world events.

Grant suggested that Europe, therefore, needs to reconcile the French and British approaches to the United States in order to develop coherent and unified foreign and defense policies. Toward that end, he favors "a stronger Europe that is usually supportive of U.S. policies but a Europe which can act autonomously, and which, on matters of vital importance, is capable of opposing the U.S."

Both the new president of the European Commission, Barroso of Portugal, and the EU foreign policy chief, Solana of Spain, are considered pro-American leaders.

Europe Takes Charge

By Andrew Moravcsik
Newsweek, July 5, 2004

Hundreds of thousands of American tourists flock to Ireland every year seeking ruined castles, green fields, and friendly folk. On his presidential visit to the Emerald Isle, Ronald Reagan raised a beer in a local pub. Bill Clinton, despite the controversy surrounding his policies on Northern Ireland, was welcomed by cheering crowds.

Not so President George W. Bush. One might have expected him to launch a week of transatlantic diplomacy, starting with the annual EU–U.S. summit on the Emerald Isle, with a popular touch. Yet Bush is now so conspicuously unpopular abroad that even in fervently pro-American Ireland, his presence creates chaos. Thousands of protesters took to the streets. Holed up in remote and romantic Dromoland Castle Hotel outside Shannon, the visiting president was defended by the largest security operation in Irish history. (Quite a distinction in a country that has faced decades of domestic terrorism.) Half the 500 members of the presidential entourage were U.S. Secret Service agents, armed with high-powered weapons, armor-piercing munitions, and bombproof cars. All this security for only a couple of hours of actual meetings with EU leaders.

U.S. officials have instead pinned their hopes on the second stop in Bush's European tour, the NATO summit in Istanbul on June 28 and 29. Bush is staying longer in Turkey, doing more talking, and hopes to get more done. The primary focus is to persuade America's European allies to contribute more military forces to U.S. efforts in Iraq. For several months, senior administration officials' briefings on NATO have spoken of little else.

Yet this effort is futile. Only the British and Poles maintain a significant number of troops in Iraq; a dozen other NATO allies have sent symbolic contingents. Germany, France, and other recalcitrant governments have signaled their unwillingness to do more than contribute to the training of Iraqi forces in third countries. None of this will change this week. The Bush administration will point to a joint communique and claim multilateral support. Americans will pen essays on the crisis of NATO and wonder why Europe lacks stronger military forces. Europeans will criticize Bush's newfound multilateralism as too little, too late—suspiciously resembling a series of photo ops designed to counter criticism from Democratic presidential candidate John Kerry that the Bush administration's unilateralist policies have alienated U.S. allies. Iraq is too controversial to generate much allied support.

In part, this failure reflects the political predicament of the Bush administration, which is desperate to shore up its controversial Iraq policy, even at the expense of pursuing more promising areas for NATO cooperation, such as Afghanistan. Yet the deeper problem is NATO itself. In a world where homeland security, nation-building, and international legitimacy are increasingly important, particularly in European eyes, NATO seems an anachronistic military defense organization constructed to oppose Soviet forces, and retains something of the static cast of Cold War deterrence.

This feeling is accentuated by the fact that the political initiative has shifted to the other Brussels-based organization: the European Union. In economic matters, it is already universally recognized that the EU is a trade-policy superpower. When the top U.S. trade official, Robert Zoellick, meets his European Commission counter-

---

It is less well recognized, particularly in the United States, that the EU has now moved . . . into foreign and defense policy.

---

part, Pascal Lamy, they bargain as equals. And when they reach an agreement, the rest of the world listens.

But it is less well recognized, particularly in the United States, that the EU has now moved far beyond economics—in particular, into foreign and defense policy. More than 80 percent of European positions in the United Nations are now coordinated, and a coherent defense identity is slowly emerging.

To be sure, NATO is and will remain the logistical basis of most Western military cooperation. More coherent multinational units are being created within NATO. It has successfully met the challenge issued by its former leader, Lord George Robertson, to "go out of area or out of business," and lent its name and a significant number of troops to operations in Kosovo and Afghanistan. This is no small achievement—and, for that, NATO remains indispensable.

Yet NATO is no longer—if indeed it ever was—a source of political initiative and legitimacy. When I toured NATO headquarters a few weeks ago, the mood was depressed, even despondent. Officials were hard-pressed to name any specific NATO contribution to the war on terrorism beyond troops in Afghanistan, some interdiction ships in the Mediterranean, and a chemical decontamination unit. More important, NATO no longer commands the sort of instinctive legitimacy among European political elites that it once enjoyed.

The emergence of the EU means that the real dynamism in transatlantic relations no longer lies in the NATO summit, but in the EU–U.S. summit. Here there is much more of which to boast. Consider the following achievements in European–U.S. relations:

- EU soldiers have begun replacing NATO forces in Bosnia. This force, eventually to total 7,000 men, is the first EU military deployment anywhere in the world.

- Britain, France, and Germany came together to forge a common policy of diplomatic and economic engagement with Iran, developed in cooperation with the United States. The results so far are debatable, but its aim—a "carrot" alongside the "stick" of a potential U.S. military strike to dismantle Iran's nuclear program—is laudable.

- U.S. Customs inspectors will expand their presence at European ports to intensify the search for bombs, chemicals, or other terrorist tampering with containers shipped to the United States.

- The new EU global positioning system, Galileo, will be coordinated with the existing American system, GPS, so that they are interoperable, frequencies do not clash, and military security is not compromised.

- EU governments will share detailed transatlantic-air-passenger lists with U.S. officials in real time to screen for potential criminal activity and security threats. Controversial issues of privacy under European law had to be overcome to reach an agreement.

U.S.–EU initiatives have moved forward in many other areas, such as intelligence sharing, coordination of HIV/AIDS programs, and efforts to promote political reform in the Middle East. Europeans and Americans have also come close to agreement on opening EU and U.S. air-transport markets to each others' airlines, though a pact remains stalled due to protectionist pressures on both sides of the Atlantic.

The EU's high representative, Javier Solana, already plays an increasingly important role in coordinating national policies. If the EU Constitution is ratified—and probably even if it is not—his diplomatic position will be consolidated into something already being referred to in Brussels as an EU "foreign minister." And, perhaps even more important, the EU—for all the Euroskeptic hoopla in the recent Europarliamentary elections—enjoys greater legitimacy among Europeans than NATO. All this will further consolidate the EU's leading role in transatlantic relations.

Little of this will actually be discussed in detail by national leaders this week and even less will appear in press reports. There is nothing sexy about container shipping, passenger lists, or peacekeeping. Nearly all the reporting will focus on NATO, and most of that on the failure, once again, to reach agreement on Iraq. Yet the core of transatlantic cooperation does not lie in presidential polemics and photo ops, but in the permanent network of transatlantic meetings between various federal agencies and their EU counterparts. In the long term, the quiet diplomacy underlying the EU–U.S. relationship may contribute far more to transatlantic welfare and security than NATO's bickering and bombast.

EU "Must Work with U.S. As an Ally"

BY TONY HELM
DAILY TELEGRAPH (LONDON), OCTOBER 15, 2004

Tony Blair demanded an end to the decades-old Franco-German domination of Europe yesterday as he called for the EU to forge a "common agenda" with the United States to solve the world's problems.

He suggested there was a danger that this year's eastward enlargement of the EU could open fresh divisions if the community's founding members did not accept new countries from the former communist East as equals.

Mr. Blair wrote in a joint newspaper article with Ferenc Gyurcsány, the Hungarian prime minister: "It's up to the old members to demonstrate to the new that the EU now also belongs to them. They must show the newcomers they are welcome."

His comments were a clear dig at President Jacques Chirac, who last year told the east European newcomers to "shut up" and listen to the EU's great powers.

Mr. Blair told a conference of centre-left leaders in Budapest that it was essential to build an outward-looking Europe of "equal partners" which regarded America as an ally rather than a "rival."

In a clear warning to Paris and Berlin against pushing ahead with integration on a fast track, he said: "We should reject any suggestion of inner or outer cores of Europe. The point of enlargement is unity not the creation of new divisions in place of those which we have erased. Together we are all founding members of a new Europe. Our future should be as one Europe where all are equal partners together."

Mr. Blair's comments in *Nepszabadsag* newspaper reflect his belief that Europe could split again if some countries pursue political and economic integration at a faster pace than the rest are prepared to accept.

The prime minister, who like many east European EU leaders is still stung by arguments with France and Germany over the war in Iraq, fears these divisions would be worsened by competing views among EU states about future relationship with America. He said: "I do believe it is essential that Europe and the United States work together. Any idea that we can build a coherent international agenda on a division between Europe and the U.S. is simply wrong.

"We need the two of them working together. Now that requires both to reach out one to the other so that we can develop that common agenda."

In a world where the problems faced by governments were global, including terrorism, trade, and the environment, the EU had to widen its horizons and seek solutions in partnership with Washington.

"We can deal with these international issues far more easily if we have a broad and simple common agenda that covers not just terrorism and WMD but also global poverty, sustainable development, the Middle East, and the modernisation of our international institutions."

Allies of Mr. Blair said he wanted to ensure that the 10 new member states who joined the EU in May—eight of them former communist nations—felt part of a pro-Atlanticist club and not inferiors in an elitist inward-looking community.

Mr. Blair also chose the Budapest meeting to demand that the EU modernise its economy and abandon its reliance on heavily regulated labour markets based on the post-war social model.

A More Perfect Union?

By Sam Natapoff
The American Prospect, September 2004

The Iraq War has quietly but fundamentally changed the course of the European Union. If in recent years Britain, France, and Germany—the EU's three most important states—had created a delicate and unprecedented harmony over Europe's future, Britain's decision to join the war destroyed it. This dissension is playing out all over Europe: French senatorial elections this month will articulate visceral anti-Americanism that calls for combating U.S. power with EU centralization, and this America-bashing has further distanced Britain from its neighbors.

Due to its importance, history, and position as Europe's financial capital, Britain is vital to the European Union's future. Yet Britain has always been ambivalent about European unity because of its centuries-long attachment to the idea of "splendid isolation." In 1955, an early British EU negotiator reportedly offered the classic British view of EU institutions: "Gentlemen, you are trying to negotiate something you will never be able to negotiate. But if negotiated, it will not be ratified. And if ratified, it will not work." In addition to this skepticism over Europe, Britain has also repeatedly chosen its "special relationship" with the United States over a more intimate relationship with the European Union.

Prime Minister Tony Blair was the first British leader to fully commit to Europe. In 1997, he rejected the traditional disdain, declaring Britain's future to be in leading a united Europe. Defying the conventional wisdom of a majority of his countrymen and political colleagues, Blair favors adoption of the new European currency and has quietly advanced EU integration at home, which surprised Britons and delighted his EU counterparts.

The Iraq War changed everything. By supporting George W. Bush and sending troops, Blair implicitly reneged on his commitment to EU unity, choosing the traditional Washington alliance over the wishes of his new allies in Paris and Berlin. As German foreign minister Joschka Fischer explained, "We all know that this is about the question of Iraq, but it's also about the question of Europe." This decision was strongly opposed at home; it severely damaged Blair's domestic position and undermined his credibility with the British people. As a result, his ability to pursue further EU integration has been sharply and perhaps irrevocably curtailed. It is ironic that Blair, Britain's most "European" prime minister, has had his electoral and political future irreparably damaged attempting to maintain Britain's special relationship across the Atlantic over a war in the Middle East.

Given Blair's striking Europeanist commitment, his support of the United States and not the European Union regarding Iraq represents a serious setback for EU development in general. As none of Blair's potential successors in either major British party is as committed to EU integration as he is, his political debilitation may be a real obstacle to further EU progress. This renewed intra-EU hostility has already had significant European political ramifications. French president Jacques Chirac aggressively opposed the Iraq War and called eastern European states "childish" and "irresponsible" for supporting it. A February 2003 poll showed that more than three-quarters of the French people considered his actions "courageous," and Chirac was short-listed for the 2003 Nobel Peace Prize. German chancellor Gerhard Schröder won a narrow re-election victory in 2002 on the Iraq issue, explicitly refusing to take part in any U.S. military "adventures," and at a June 2004 EU summit, he shouted to Blair that their relationship was "finished."

These hostilities have had explicit consequences for recent EU negotiations. First, in talks about a new EU constitution, finalized in June 2004, British officials had initially appeared committed to the larger European project. After Iraq, however, these negotiators appeared far more skeptical, demanding opt-out clauses over asylum, migration, and judicial policies in an attempt to protect Britain from the treaty rather than to commit to it. These disagreements became public in June when Chirac and Schröder attacked Blair for putting Britain's national interests before European interests, with Chirac accusing Blair of thwarting the constitution's very goal of moving toward ever-closer integration and ending the veto as a device to block progress. Britain responded that decisions over Europe's future had to be made by all 25 EU members, not by "six or two [Germany and France] or one [France]."

The new constitution's main achievement had been to extend qualified majority voting (allocating EU voting power based on a nation's population size rather than simply one vote per country) to several areas of European policy, rather than requiring unanimity. Britain, however, prevented the extension of this broader voting arrangement to key spheres including taxation, defense, and foreign policy, thus maintaining a veto in these areas for every EU state and preventing the constitution from becoming more wide-ranging. For example, the constitution allows for a European public prosecutor, but as a result of (mainly) British objections, he or she is limited to investigating fraud regarding EU funds, and cannot investigate other serious cross-border criminal cases.

The EU constitution, however, was not the only point of contention. In June 2004, Britain squared off with France and Germany again over the selection of the next president of the European Commission—the EU's executive branch. Britain's candidate called for a European Union of more circumscribed powers, while France and Germany's candidate had a far more centralized and expansive view. Both sides vetoed the other's choice. A hostile stalemate prevailed, and several more candidates were rejected until Portugal's José Barroso was reluctantly accepted as the least offensive candidate to both sides, nicknamed "Mr. Nobody" by British tabloids.

The Iraq War also polarized Turkey's application for EU membership. Prior to the war, Turkey's application hinged on several issues, including sufficient progress on human rights and the judiciary, as well as several EU members' reluctance to integrate a Muslim state into the union. Already delicate, the membership negotiation was made more controversial when the government of Turkey, a NATO member and a traditional U.S. ally, initially offered to let Bush use Turkish bases in case of war with Iraq, incensing the anti-war EU states (the Turkish parliament vetoed the offer). Thereafter, in June 2004, Bush publicly called upon the European Union to accept Turkey's application. This enraged Chirac, who publicly told Bush to mind his own business. Today, Britain and the United States support Turkey's application as a longtime ally, while France and Germany reportedly still have reservations.

With the end of the Cold War, the United States began to see the European Union more as a competitor than an ally.

This EU schism cannot be laid at Britain's doorstep alone, though. The United States played a key role in creating it, both by invading Iraq and, more generally, by its shift in attitude. The U.S. view of European unity has had a long and complicated history. Following World War II and with the Soviet Union looming, the United States saw the nascent European Union as a bulwark against instability, and it supported the Franco-German efforts to create new European institutions. In addition to the munificence of the Marshall Plan, in 1952, Secretary of State Dean Acheson expressed the strong U.S. support that "the political and economic unification of Europe warrants."

However, with the end of the Cold War, the United States began to see the European Union more as a competitor than an ally, a process President Bush has accelerated. His increasing willingness to choose unilateral action over multilateral action found expression in withdrawing the United States from the Kyoto Protocol, the International Criminal Court, the Anti-Ballistic Missile Treaty, and the Nuclear Test Ban Treaty. During a 2003 press conference, Defense Secretary Donald Rumsfeld gave a speech that divided the European Union into "old Europe" (France and Germany) and "new Europe" (Atlanticists) on the question of invading Iraq. Cherishing their independence, many EU states considered this an act of insensitive U.S. intervention in internal EU affairs that ignored the union's overall integrity.

This rupture may pose near-term problems for the EU's future. But it also represents an opportunity. The old powerhouses Britain, France, and Germany—are now facing a structural challenge from a more responsive and democratic Europe. The days of tripartite domination are over. As a result of the new constitution, future EU decisions will require the agreement of more than half the EU member countries, not simply a few. The new constitution has markedly reduced both Britain's ability to unilaterally prevent integration and France and Germany's capacity to dictate the EU's direction. In fact, the bitter dissension over the Iraq War may have illustrated not simply the rifts between the major EU states but also the way forward for the EU as an evolving whole.

Transatlantic Divides

BY WEN STEPHENSON
BOSTON GLOBE, NOVEMBER 21, 2004

"Yes, it is a manifesto," Timothy Garton Ash said last Monday as he sat in the bar of his hotel in Kenmore Square. The Oxford historian and transatlantic commentator was referring to his new book, *Free World: America, Europe, and the Surprising Future of the West* (Random House). "It is an attempt," he said, "to wake people up, and to say, 'The world is not safe in this lot's hands. And you can make a difference.'"

The genre is a notable departure for Garton Ash, 49, whose previous books have documented the upheavals in central and eastern Europe with a combination of eyewitness reportage and keen historical analysis—what the diplomat George Kennan, reviewing Garton Ash's *The Uses of Adversity* (1989), called "history of the present." And yet this manifesto isn't likely to spur people into the streets. It's far too nicely reasoned, and reasonable, for that.

His purpose, Garton Ash writes in the new book, is "to chip away at the mind-walls of prejudice and constructed difference between Europe and America." He argues forcefully, though always politely, against both the Bush administration's unilateralism and against those who would have Europe become a superpower to rival the United States. ("The Chiracian version of Euro-Gaullism leads nowhere," he writes.) Our present situation, says Garton Ash, is simply far too dangerous to allow divisions between and within Western democracies to distract us from urgent crises in the Middle East, from global warming, and from crippling poverty and disease in the developing world. If we don't get these things right, he warns—and we can only do so together—the epitaph on the West's gravestone may read: 'They squabbled as the Earth burned.'" —Wen Stephenson

***Ideas* [section of the *Boston Globe*]:** Colin Powell has announced his resignation as secretary of state. How did he play in Europe?

Garton Ash: Well, he played extremely well—literally played. If you have seen David Hare's play, *Stuff Happens*, about the diplomacy surrounding the Iraq crisis—which was a terrific hit in London—the absolute hero of that play is none other than Colin

Powell. He is the only unambiguously sympathetic character. . . . If he's gone and Rumsfeld stays, that would be read, rightly or wrongly, as a signal of the Bush administration's intentions.

Ideas: What is the European reaction to Condoleezza Rice as Powell's successor?

Garton Ash: The reaction is, "Let's wait and see." She's been interpreted as not unambiguously for or against the administration's approach to Europe. . . . So I think it's good news. She does have a very sophisticated understanding of international affairs, and a very good understanding of the British position, not least because of her connections to the British government. It's remarkable that she recently celebrated her 50th birthday at the residence of the British ambassador in Washington, with the president in attendance.

Ideas: You met with President Bush at the White House in May 2001. How did that come about?

Garton Ash: It was the most extraordinary thing. I was sitting in my office in Oxford, and I get a telephone call, and someone says, "It's the White House here, could you come and tell President Bush about Europe, uh, next Thursday at 1:45?" So, I said, "Well, I do have a lunch, but if I can move it. . . ."

Ideas: What was the meeting like?

Garton Ash: We were a group of specialists on Europe—three Americans, two Brits, no French, no Germans—and the president was clearly feeling his way, very much sure of himself on some issues like missile defense and the environment—"Kyoto is mush," he said—and not on others. . . . But I'll never forget one thing he said, very emphatically, "Do we want the European Union to succeed?" And my British colleague and I said that we certainly did, and we thought the United States should, too. And then he sort of stepped back and said, "That was just a provocation." But actually, I thought that probably not a single president since 1945 would have asked the question in that form.

Ideas: You write that when you see how foreign policy decisions are made, "you are left with a sense of mild incredulity that this is how the world is run."

Garton Ash: It's an almighty mess. . . . It's amazing on what little knowledge, and what prejudices, our leaders make their decisions. . . . The diplomacy of the Iraq crisis was a case study of how not to run a world, with terrible mistakes made on all sides, in Washington, Paris and London, Berlin, Beijing.

Ideas: Would a different generation of leaders have done better?

Garton Ash: Yes, I actually do think that. An earlier generation— Churchill, Roosevelt, Truman, Adenauer, De Gaulle—had gone through certain very formative experiences. Our leaders, who are

40-something to early 50s, are professional politicians who haven't done much else in their lives and often don't have much international experience. And it shows.

Ideas: You write of the U.S.-Europe divide over Iraq as a "crisis of the West." Yet is it possible that Europeans have this sense of a crisis and Americans don't?

Garton Ash: Perhaps many Americans are less inclined than Europeans to think that it matters so much. You know, I can have a crisis with my cleaning lady, but I don't think that matters as much as the crisis with my wife. So is Europe the wife or the cleaning lady?

Ideas: There's another analogy—Europe as the jilted lover.

Garton Ash: Yes. America spends its time talking about America. Europe spends its time talking about— America.

Ideas: It's not good, they should really get over us.

> *"America spends its time talking about America. Europe spends its time talking about— America."*—
> **Timothy Garton Ash**

Garton Ash: Well, that's part of American soft power—and it's part of American hyperpower, too. Everyone is fascinated by what's going on here. . . . A very important example is Germany. We talk so much about France, but the one that matters more is Germany. And Germany, which was of course liberated, occupied by America, and became extremely Americanized, feels that its love has not been requited, that it's been spurned.

Ideas: Is Turkey going to be invited into the EU?

Garton Ash: I hope so, because it will send a very important signal to the whole Islamic world, that a country with a secular state but an Islamist government has a place in one of the main clubs of the West.

Ideas: Does this create divisions in Europe over what is "European"?

Garton Ash: People often say what's at issue here is, "Is Europe a Christian club?" But you could equally well say that what's at issue here is, "Is Europe a secular club?" Because a strong part of the ideology of most people who support the European project is the notion of secularism . . . indeed, they are secularist to the core. In other words, their objection to Turkey is the same as their objection to America.

Ideas: One wonders if Europeans really understand the debate over religion and politics in America.

Garton Ash: There are aspects of American religiosity that are baffling. Sitting in a cab the other day, I listened to Family Radio, and the announcer is seriously discussing a book, *Did God Have a Plan for America?* And the answer is "Yes, He did."

Ideas: Of course, it was an Englishman who gave us that idea.

Garton Ash: Oh? Which one?

Ideas: Well, you go back to the Puritans and John Winthrop.

Garton Ash: The Puritans, oh, yes, the City on a Hill! But that was the 17th century, and we're now in the 21st.

Ideas: How far apart, really, are the U.S. and Europe?

Garton Ash: In some respects, the Atlantic is narrower than the English Channel. I think the divide is much more in mutual perceptions than it is in reality. But perceptions can become reality. And if we go on thinking of each other as the "other" for a few more years, then that can become so.

Ideas: And what's at stake in that?

Garton Ash: I would say what's at stake is genuinely the future of freedom. If we duck these big challenges because we're involved in these absurd squabbles, what Freud called "the narcissism of minor differences," then the world will be a much more dangerous and nasty place for our children in 20 years.

VI. Environmental Policy

Editor's Introduction

One of the ways in which the European Union differs from the United States is in its handling of environmental issues. "Green" political parties hold seats in many European parliaments, as well as the European Parliament, so a fair degree of activism can be expected. In August 2004 the EU's Environment Agency released a study of the probable impact of global warming that was, as Gareth Harding reports for United Press International, a "Doomsday Climate Warning for the EU." Because of its long, indented coastline with rivers that penetrate far into the interior, its dense population, and its very diverse regional climates, Europe is peculiarly vulnerable to rising temperatures and rising sea levels, as well as to the violent weather events that are thought to accompany global warming. If the gradual inundation of Venice and the emergence of a prehistoric corpse from a melting glacier hadn't already convinced many Europeans that global warming was under way, the floods and record-breaking heat waves of the past few years would have done so.

Support for the Kyoto Protocol, a pioneering international agreement to slow the build-up of greenhouse gases, is strong in Europe, but action could not be taken until a sufficient number of industrial nations had ratified the treaty. As Peter N. Spotts reports in "Emissions Pact Goes Forward," from the *Christian Science Monitor*, that line was crossed when Russia finally agreed to the protocol, whereupon the European Union entered into a complex carbon-emissions trading scheme based on a similar plan used to reduce sulfur dioxide pollution in California. The trading system, expected to benefit both Russia and the Union, will also be a first step toward reducing the production of greenhouse gases worldwide.

In "Bigger EU Could Affect Environmental Policies," from *Environmental Science & Technology*, Maria Burke points out that many of the new member states have extensive and expensive environmental problems, the legacy of untrammeled development under Soviet rule, and no funds to pay for repairs or clean-up. Really innovative environmental projects are likely to remain on the drawing board, Burke thinks, while the Union addresses the needs of Eastern Europe, probably favoring market-based approaches so as not to disrupt the economies of the new member states too suddenly. There is, she says, support for environmental action within the new member states, though little chance of meeting all the EU's deadlines. A sidebar, "EU's Natural Gems," from Reuters via the magazine *Environment*, observes that the Soviet practice of grouping heavy industries together in one place has left some areas of Eastern Europe in remarkably pristine condition, even while others are an ecological nightmare.

Finally, in "Europe Is United: No Bioengineered Food" from the *International Herald Tribune*, Elisabeth Rosenthal describes the EU opposition to the genetically modified foods that Americans buy and consume every day. Popular resistance is so strong that even after the EU bowed to American pressure and removed some legal restrictions on the sale of these foods, grocers saw no point in giving them shelf space, for the public was simply not going to buy them. As Rosenthal explains, this is a billion-dollar impasse, affecting trade between the EU and the United States and the EU and Africa, and it seems to have taken American companies by surprise. Despite the constant bickering and bargaining within the EU, there are times when Europe does speak with one voice, and then it can pay to listen.

Doomsday Climate Warning for EU

By Gareth Harding
United Press International, August 19, 2004

Melting glaciers, higher sea levels, increased flooding, soaring temperatures, falling crop harvests, and more devastating storms—it sounds like the synopsis of the blockbuster movie *The Day After Tomorrow,* in which downtown Manhattan is buried in 30-storey snowdrifts and a 100-foot tidal wave engulfs the Statue of Liberty.

In fact, these are among the effects of climate change that are already being felt in Europe or are likely to happen over the coming decades, according to a new EU report.

Drawn up by the European Environment Agency, the study paints a bleak picture of continental climate changes in the first half of the 21st century. It says the concentration of carbon dioxide, the main greenhouse gas, is at its highest level in Europe for at least 420,000 years and has risen by more than a third since the Industrial Revolution.

"The extent and rate of the climate changes under way most likely exceed all natural variation in climate over the last thousand years and possibly longer," says the report, drawn up by a Europe-wide team of scientists. Noting that the 1990s were the warmest decade on record and that the three hottest years in history—1998, 2002, and 2003—have occurred in the last six years, it claims Europe is warming faster than any other continent.

The United Nations' Intergovernmental Panel on Climate Change suggests the average global temperature could be between 1.4 and 5.8 degrees Celsius warmer in 2100 than in 1990. But the EEA study estimates that over the past 100 years, the temperature in Europe has risen by an average of 0.95 degrees Celsius and is projected to climb by a further 2.0 to 6.3 degrees by the end of this century if the build-up of greenhouse gas emissions continues unabated.

The effects are already being felt. Glaciers are in retreat and are at their lowest levels for 5,000 years; sea levels in Europe—which rose by 0.03–0.12 inches a year in the 20th century—are projected to rise at two to four times this speed during the current century, and by 2080 cold winters could disappear almost entirely as the continent heats up, the report predicts.

"This is a phenomenon that will considerably affect our societies and environments for decades and centuries to come," said EEA director Prof. Jacqueline McGlade in a statement.

The Copenhagen-based research body could not have picked a better time to launch the study, with northwest Europe battered by high winds and torrential rains. Last year, a prolonged heat wave on the continent led to 20,000 deaths, sharply reduced crop yields, and shrinking glaciers; while in 2002 flooding in central Europe killed 80 people and left tens of thousands homeless.

McGlade rightly points out that "climate change is no longer an environmental issue but a hot topic for finance ministers and their treasuries." During the 1990s, the average number of weather-related disasters doubled compared with the previous 10 years, racking up annual losses of around $11 billion annually.

But it is not all doom and gloom. Rising temperatures could benefit farmers in northern Europe, allowing them to grow more profitable crops for longer periods—although parts of southern Europe

---

"Climate change is no longer an environmental issue but a hot topic for finance ministers and their treasuries."—Jacqueline McGlade, EEA director

---

could be turned into a dust bowl by the same process. Warmer weather could also lead to lower greenhouse gas emissions as less energy is needed to heat homes.

But overall, the 110-page study is a wakeup call to Europe's politicians to turn their lofty climate change rhetoric into action. Under the Kyoto Protocol, which was signed in 1997, the EU is committed to reducing its emissions of six greenhouse gases by 8 percent between 1990 and 2012.

EEA figures released last month showed a slight drop in discharges of 0.5 percent between 2001 and 2002. But with EU-15 emissions down by less than 3 percent since 1990, the bloc still has a long way to go to meet its international targets. "Kyoto is not enough to prevent a rapid increase in carbon dioxide emissions, but that should not stop us adopting strategies to deal with the effects of climate change now," McGlade told United Press International.

While the EU wrestles with how to stem the damage caused by climate change, the U.S government is still arguing whether there is any evidence of such change, and Russia is still weighing up the pros and cons of signing the Kyoto treaty. For the protocol to enter into effect, at least one of these two countries has to sign up, although the likelihood of President George W. Bush's administration doing so is about as remote as snow falling in the Sahara desert.

The vast majority of Europeans believe climate change is real, its effects are being felt now, and radical action is needed to cut greenhouse gas emissions. But not everyone is convinced that alarm bells should be ringing. Writing in Britain's *Daily Telegraph* newspaper shortly before the release of *The Day After Tomorrow*, Bjorn Lomborg—the controversial Danish author of *The Skeptical Environmentalist*—argued: "Implementing the Kyoto agreement on climate change would cost at least $150 billion each year, yet would do no more than postpone global warming for six years by 2100."

No one doubts that curbing greenhouse gas emissions is an expensive business, but most Europeans argue the costs of doing nothing—both financially and in environmental terms—would be much greater in the long term. "Europe cannot afford to have such events as the Danube flooding two years ago, which cost at least 15 billion euros," says McGlade. "That's not the sort of 'Day After Tomorrow' we want."

Emissions Pact Goes Forward

By Peter N. Spotts
The Christian Science Monitor, October 7, 2004

After seven years of bruising negotiations, repudiation by one of its early architects, and repeated pronouncements of its imminent demise, a 1997 pact to curb the growth of greenhouse gases tied to global warming is limping toward ratification.

Now comes the hard part: putting its complex rules into effect, and planning for what will follow once the agreement's first—and so far, only—formal commitment period ends after 2012.

"This is the most complicated, sophisticated effort at directed change" in international environmental policy ever attempted, notes Elliot Diringer, director of international strategies for the Pew Center on Global Climate Change. "Is it possible? We'll find out."

The pact in question, the 1997 Kyoto Protocol, requires countries signing the agreement to reduce global carbon-dioxide emissions by an average of 5 percent below 1990 levels by 2012.

Many atmospheric scientists agree that these emissions are at least partly responsible for an increase in average global temperatures. Those temperatures are expected to rise for the foreseeable future, with disruptive consequences worldwide.

Already, 126 nations have ratified the agreement—more than double the 55 needed. But the ratifying industrial countries only accounted for 44.2 percent of industrial-country emissions (55 percent are needed).

Last week, the final piece in that ratification puzzle appeared to fall into place when the Russian cabinet voted to ratify the accord. It now goes to the Russian Duma for the final vote, seen by many as a formality in the wake of the cabinet's decision.

Even if every signatory meets its emissions-reduction goal, the effort would barely slow the rate of increase of CO_2 and have virtually no effect on climate.

By the end of this century, atmospheric CO_2 is expected to double over preindustrial levels. That's because of the world's widespread use of coal, oil, and natural gas since the start of the Industrial Revolution as well as changes in land-use patterns.

Yet the value of the agreement lies less in its immediate effect on the atmosphere than on the political and diplomatic chemistry needed to deal with a problem that is likely to take decades to solve, some analysts say.

The 1997 accord "puts real pressure on countries to deliver on their commitments. Countries will demonstrate that it can be done affordably. And most important, ratification sets in motion the diplomatic machinery" to look beyond 2012, Mr. Diringer says.

He notes that the accord requires signatories to begin talks next year on a new round of targets and timetables for emission reductions.

"This is the first step in what will need to be a decades-long process," adds David Sandalow, a Brookings Institution scholar who has served as assistant secretary of state for oceans, environment, and science under President Clinton.

A Trading Scheme

By most accounts, the European Union is in the vanguard of efforts to implement the Kyoto accords. The EU has set up a carbon-emissions trading scheme, which takes effect in January, according to David Victor, director of the Program on Energy and Sustainable Development at Stanford University in Palo Alto, Calif. In addition, it has developed a set of voluntary and binding regulations to cover households, transportation, and the building sector.

By most accounts, the European Union is in the vanguard of efforts to implement the Kyoto accords.

The EU is likely to fall a little short in meeting its Kyoto targets on its own, he says, but Russia's participation will come to Europe's rescue.

Because the Russian economy was in such shambles in 1990, the base line against which Kyoto targets are measured, Moscow's emissions targets are far above existing emissions. So Russia has carbon "credits" it can sell to EU members.

European countries can also earn credit against their emissions targets for helping Russia build cleaner, more efficient power plants and factories. Such "joint implementation" projects, permitted under Kyoto's ground rules, are expected to allow the EU to claim victory in meeting its targets by 2012.

Other industrial countries, such as Canada and Japan, are further behind. Japan's biggest problem is emissions from autos, notes Philip Clapp, president of the National Environmental Trust, an environmental group in Washington, D.C. Three years ago, the country tried to lay plans for higher domestic fuel-economy standards to meet its Kyoto commitments, Mr. Clapp says, but the U.S. threatened to challenge those standards before the World Trade Organization. Japan's move would constitute a trade barrier against American auto imports, the U.S. argued.

Now, analysts say, Japan is said to be exploring an internal carbon-trading system, as well as taxes on emissions to help it meet its Kyoto targets.

In the end, Clapp says, "the countries that have ratified will comply" using the full range of mechanisms the pact makes available.

The big question, he continues, is what happens after 2012.

Getting the U.S. to Join

Next year, talks are set to begin on a post-2012 emissions-control regime. A key goal is likely to be a hunt for ways to get countries, including China and the United States, to buy in to a new agreement. That will require thinking outside the 1997 protocol box, some analysts say.

The challenge will be to overcome the inertia that could build behind Kyoto's existing mechanisms if they prove successful during the first commitment period. "When a model is seen as effective, it's hard to swim against the tide," Dr. Victor says.

Bigger EU Could Affect Environmental Policies

By Maria Burke
Environmental Science & Technology, September 1, 2004

Will an expanded European Union continue to pursue aggressive environmental policies? With 10 new member states—many with significant environmental problems and limited funds to tackle them—joining the EU, experts expect major impacts on policy. Some predict that EU environmental policy will stagnate as the new states struggle to implement and comply with Western Europe's much tougher regulations. Others say that future EU policies could tend to more market-based approaches rather than old-fashioned command-and-control laws.

EU's newest members, which joined the Union in late May and raised the total membership to 25, are Cyprus, Czech Republic, Estonia, Hungary, Latvia, Lithuania, Malta, Poland, Slovakia, and Slovenia.

The new states "have less of a tradition of environmental management and could exert a downward pull on the existing [member states]," says Miranda Schreurs, a political scientist at the University of Maryland. "For the next 5 to 10 years, the EU will probably focus on implementing existing legislation rather than pushing forward with yet more progressive laws," she adds.

Despite dramatic improvement in air and water quality in many former Soviet bloc countries in Central and Eastern Europe—mainly because of economic reform and the closing of inefficient factories—substantial problems remain, particularly in Czech Republic and Poland. For example, while these states have moved away from heavily polluting industrial and energy plants, they still depend heavily on coal. And the Baltic states of Estonia, Latvia, and Lithuania lack adequate waste disposal facilities and suffer from illegal waste dumping.

Andrew Farmer of the Institute for European Environment Policy in London suggests that the new states could put a hold on policy advances. "It's not likely that new [member states] will sign up to more legislation or be a major driver of future legislation, and they could drag the whole EU back," Farmer argues. He points out that if the new states stick together, or team up with small states such as Portugal, they could block a decision in the Environment

---

EU's Natural Gems

ENVIRONMENT, JULY/AUGUST 2004

The newest members of the European Union (EU)—Poland, Hungary, the Czech and Slovak Republics, and the three Baltic states—bring a wealth of naturally preserved lands with them but will still need to make large investments in water and waste management to comply with EU standards. Rich in wildlife, this area in central and eastern Europe is home to about one-fifth of Europe's forests, as well as several animal species that are slowly dying in western Europe. While the countries abound with unique river valleys, sand dunes, and fauna, the marks of a former industry-intensive communist territory—ravaged forests, polluted rivers, and toxic chemical–producing smokestacks—are still visible. "Communism had a paradoxical impact," says Andreas Beckmann, EU accession coordinator at the Worldwide Fund for Nature's Austrian office. "The top-down, centrally controlled system . . . destroyed areas like the Black Triangle but there are other areas where no development was concentrated. As a result, they were relatively preserved." Beckmann noted that water and waste management would top the list of environmental concerns for the new EU members, adding that it would take these countries another decade to meet EU water standards. Experts say to comply with EU environmental laws and standards, the newcomers will have to invest up to $141.7 billion, and the cleanup could take as many as 12 years to complete. Despite these drawbacks—and the fear that new road and factory construction projects will overshadow environmental concerns—the European Commission says that the new EU countries have made considerable progress in improving their landscapes.

Environment, volume 46, number 6, pages 8–9, July/August 2004. Reprinted with permission of the Helen Dwight Reid Educational Foundation. Published by Heldref Publications, 1319 Eighteenth St., NW, Washington, DC 20036-1802. Copyright © 2004.

Council of Ministers, the final arbiter in the law-making process. "This gives them a very strong negotiating position if they all agree."

It also seem clear that the enlarged EU will further embrace market-based approaches rather than standards and deadlines, says Jacqueline Karas of the Royal Institute of International Affairs in London. The new members tend to be pro-business and anti-regulation because of their communist pasts, creating a stronger voice for market-based mechanisms in new areas such as water quality, she predicts. At the same time, these accession states also could be a good testing ground for new policy instruments, Schreurs adds, such as voluntary agreements for eco-labeling and market mechanisms such as emissions trading and energy taxes.

Regardless of approach, EU enlargement is expected to bring major environmental benefits to the new member states. The accession countries, some with poor environmental protection records, have agreed to strict EU laws and must pass national laws that implement the EU's directive. "These countries, with their levels of economic development, would not have adopted this type of legislation otherwise," says Schreurs.

All the new member states have submitted step-by step implementation plans and have to report on their progress to the European Commission (EC). Officials say that the accession countries are mostly on track to implement EU environmental legislation. However, EU officials note that some countries, which they won't name, need to do "significant work" on waste management.

In the meantime, the EU has agreed to let all the new states transition to the tougher laws, mainly for regulation of water, waste, and industrial pollution. These transitional plans differ by country and include legally binding and non-negotiable intermediate targets and deadlines. For example, Latvia and Hungary have until 2015 to meet urban wastewater treatment requirements, Estonia and Lithuania must comply with air pollution requirements on large combustion plants by 2015, and Cyprus and Czech Republic are expected to meet recovery targets for packaging waste in 2005. The EC will apply its normal enforcement procedures if countries don't comply.

Karas has been surprised at the level of the new member states' progress so far and says that the governments of several countries

---

The accession countries are mostly on track to implement EU environmental legislation.

---

are trying really hard to implement the EU laws through their own national laws. Poland passed an Environmental Protection Act in 2001, for example, and set renewable energy targets to expand its share of renewable energies from 0.7% of all energy sources in 2001 to 7.5% by 2010. "But," she adds, "it remains to be seen how rapidly [the EU regulations] will happen."

Complying with EU environmental law will require significant investment. The EC estimates it will cost the 10 member states €80–110 billion in total, or on average 2–3% of the EU's gross domestic product in the coming years. The EU has been providing environmental aid since 2000 and tripled that amount in May to €8 billion, which is around 10% of the new member states' investment requirements until 2006. Other financial sources providing help include international institutions like the European Investment Bank, private groups, and consumer charges, such as fees on water and taxes.

However, current expenditures are generally well below the target amount. For example, Poland, which is the most populous of the new states, currently spends only about half the old, 15-member EU average on environmental protection, says Schreurs. "The Polish government has estimated that it must spend €40 billion— one year's total budget—in the coming years to comply with EU environmental standards," points out Schreurs. "The EU will provide perhaps €6 billion. It remains a big question where the rest will come from. Emissions trading will help, increased fuel taxes will help, but they will only make a small dent. There is reason for some of the skepticism that is out there about the ability of new member states to meet EU standards."

Most nongovernmental aid agencies agree. According to a survey of nongovernmental organizations (NGOs) in the new MS by the European Environment Bureau (EEB), an umbrella organization of environmental NGOs, inadequate funding and a lack of administrative resources are the biggest impediments to bringing about environmental and legal change. EEB's Mara Silina says the public sector cannot compete with industry when it comes to salaries for the talented people needed to build up the necessary ministries, monitoring agencies, and inspectorates. "It is a big problem that environment agencies and ministries are often small and weak," warns Schreurs. "A small number of bureaucrats must learn a vast body of law and try to implement it without adequate resources."

Europe Is United:
No Bioengineered Food

By Elisabeth Rosenthal
International Herald Tribune, October 6, 2004

Some are smokers. Some drink too much. Some admit they love red meat. But virtually all shoppers here at the Migros Supermarket on the bustling Rue des Paquis are united in avoiding a risk they regard as unacceptable: genetically modified food.

That is easy to do here in Switzerland, as in the rest of Europe, where food containing such ingredients must be labeled by law. Many large retailers, like Migros, have essentially stopped stocking the products, regarding them as bad for public image.

"I try not to eat any of it and always read the boxes," said Marco Feline, 32, an artist in jeans, getting onto his bike (with no helmet). "It scares me because we don't know what the long-term effects will be—on people or the environment."

The majority of corn and soy in the United States is now grown from genetically modified seeds, altered to increase their resistance to pests or reduce their need for water, for example. In the past decade, Americans have happily—if unknowingly—gobbled down hundreds of millions of servings of genetically modified foods. The U.S. Food and Drug Administration says there have been no adverse effects, and there is no specific labeling.

But in Europe—where food is high culture, if not religion—farmers, consumers, chefs, and environmental groups have joined voices loudly and stubbornly to oppose bioengineered foods, effectively blocking their arrival at the farms and on the tables of the Continent. And that, in turn, has created a huge ripple effect on trade and politics, from North America to Africa.

The United States, Canada, and Argentina have filed a complaint that is pending before the World Trade Organization, contending that European laws and procedures that discriminate against genetically modified products are irrational and unscientific, and so constitute an unfair trade barrier.

U.S. companies like Monsanto, which invested heavily in the technology, suffered huge losses when Europe balked. As part of a public relations effort, the U.S. State Department enlisted a Vatican academy last month as a co-sponsor of a conference in Rome, "Feeding a Hungry World: The Moral Imperative of Biotechnology."

In response to such pressure, the European Union has relaxed legal restrictions on genetically modified foods.

In May the EU approved for sale a genetically modified sweet corn, lifting a five-year moratorium on new imports. Last month the European Commission gave its seal of approval to 17 types of genetically modified corn seed for farming. But no one expects a wide-open market.

"We have no illusion that the market will change anytime soon," said Markus Payer, spokesman for Syngenta, the Swiss agribusiness company whose BT-11 corn got the approval in May. "That will only be created by consumer acceptance in Europe."

"There is currently no inclination among European consumers to buy these things," Payer went on. "But the atmosphere of rejection is not based on facts. That is a political, cultural, and media-driven decision. And so we are convinced that more and more consumers will see the benefits."

The battle lines between countries for and against genetically modified foods seem to be hardening.

Indeed, the battle lines between countries for and against genetically modified foods seem to be hardening. Several African countries, following Europe's lead, have rejected donations of genetically engineered food and seeds. In Asia, reluctance appears to be spreading. While countries like China and India are enthusiastically planting biotech crops like cotton, genetically modified food crops are having trouble winning approval.

Africa's rejection is based partly on health and local environmental concerns, but also on economic interests: Zambia and Mozambique have discovered a good market in selling unmodified grain and soy to Europe, supplanting the United States as European suppliers.

Mauro Albrizio, vice president of the European Environmental Bureau, a policy group based in Brussels, said: "In the U.S., genetically modified foods were a fait accompli; here in Europe we succeeded in preventing that."

Genetically modified foods arrived on America's dinner plates with little fanfare in the mid-1990s as large-scale farmers in the United States enthusiastically started planting the seeds, which increased production and reduced the amount of pesticide required. Convinced that bioengineered food was "at least as safe as conventional food," the U.S. Food and Drug Administration declared that a bioengineered lemon was the same as an ordinary lemon, and did not require special labeling or regulation.

Today, nearly two-thirds of the genetically modified crops in the world are grown in the United States, mostly corn and soybeans. "In the U.S., a large part of the diet is actually bioengineered," said Lester Crawford, acting commissioner of the Food and Drug agency.

"The first thing other nations want to know is how many illnesses or adverse reactions we've seen," he added. "But we haven't actually had any problems at all with bioengineered foods."

Vast amounts of money are at stake. Believing that genetically modified foods would quickly catch on throughout the world as they had in the United States, large biotech companies like Monsanto invested billions of dollars.

Since the late 1990s the European Union has required that all food containing more than tiny amounts of genetically modified materials be labeled, and that all genetically modified products be submitted for approval before sale in Europe. No products were approved during an informal moratorium from 1998 to 2003. In the past five years, many parts of Europe have enacted local bans on growing such foods.

In fact, most scientific panels have concluded that "foods derived from the transgenic crops currently on the market are safe to eat," in the words of a recent report from the UN's Food and Agricultural Organization. But the report also cautioned that crops must be evaluated case by case.

And low risk is not no risk. The 87 member states of the UN-sponsored Cartegena Protocol on Biosafety required labeling this year of all bulk shipments of food containing genetically modified products. The United States has not signed the pact.

More important, though, is that the assessment of risk depends largely on the degree of proof that a country's consumers demand.

"In their personal lives people take lots of risk—they drive too fast and bungee-jump—but for food their acceptance of risk is very low," said Philipp Hubner of the Basel-Stadt Canton Laboratory in Switzerland, which tests products in that country for contamination with genetically modified organisms. But Hubner sees his work as detecting fraud in labeling rather than as safeguarding the public health.

In late 2002, 88.6 percent of Europeans listed the "quality of food products" as an environmental issue with health implications.

"For most scientists it is not so much a safety issue, but an ethical and societal question," he said. "This is what the public here has chosen, like Muslims choosing not to eat pork."

In a survey by the European Opinion Research Group in late 2002, 88.6 percent of Europeans listed the "quality of food products" as an environmental issue with health implications.

But health fears, which can move markets, are not always consistent. In some parts of Europe, like Bordeaux, that have declared themselves free of genetically modified organisms, energy is supplied by nuclear power plants.

To sell Sugar Pops cereal to European consumers, Kellogg's imports unmodified corn from Argentina and spends extra money to make sure that the entire transportation and processing chain is free of bioengineered products, said Chris Wermann, a company spokesman. The same cereal contains genetically modified corn in the United States. Both varieties contain all the usual sugars, artificial colors and flavors.

European advocates defend their right to be finicky. "This is not ideology—it's a pragmatic stand because of potential risks to health and the environment," said Albrizio of the European Environmental Bureau, noting that there is some evidence that genetically modified crops may trigger more allergies.

In terms of agriculture, there are some very clear-cut effects, since genetically modified seeds tend to spread in the environment once they have been planted, making it hard to maintain crops that are organic and free of genetic modification. Scientists call this phenomenon "co-mixing."

To environmentalists and especially to farmers, "co-mixing" is potentially devastating "contamination." That is why the farmers of Tuscany and 11 other regions of Italy have declared themselves free of bioengineering.

In fact, European farmers and consumers have so far created a firewall against genetically modified organisms, one that the changing laws and World Trade Organization challenges may not breach easily.

"In theory you could sell GMO products here, with labeling," Hubner said. "But I'm not aware of any products that are now being sold, because no store wants them on their shelves."

Appendix

Timeline of the European Union

1914–1919: World War I. British and French governments (Allies) coordinate supplies for troops fighting German forces in France.

1939–1945: World War II.

1947–1951: In the aftermath of World War II, the United States' Marshall Plan provides $12 billion in assistance to war-ravaged Europe, mostly in the west; the Soviet-dominated nations of the east reject American aid.

1948: Attempts to form a European defense league falter, mostly because of fears of a rearmed Germany.

1949: The North Atlantic Treaty creates NATO, a military alliance between the United States and the countries of Western Europe, pledging mutual defense in case of Soviet aggression.

1951: Treaty of Paris. Six European nations—France, West Germany, Italy, Belgium, the Netherlands, and Luxembourg—agree to combine mining and manufacturing resources in the European Coal and Steel Community (ECSC). By this action they hope to prevent competition over the coal-rich Ruhr Valley from developing into another European war; they also hope to facilitate economic recovery. The ECSC is the brainchild of Jean Monnet, a French economic consultant and longtime advocate of international cooperation (he will become the first president of the independent board that governs the ECSC). French foreign minister Robert Schuman and German chancellor Konrad Adenauer support the plan, officially proposed by Schuman on May 9, 1950.

1957: The Treaties of Rome 1) create a European Atomic Energy Community (Euratom) to control and share the development of nuclear energy and 2) further integrate the economies of the six nations in what becomes the European Economic Community (EEC). The six nations begin to remove trade barriers and work toward a common market.

1959: First reduction of customs duties.

1960s: The EEC flourishes. Great Britain twice (1963 and 1967) applies for membership but is blackballed by French leader Charles de Gaulle, who fears that Britain, with its close ties to the United States, may be a stalking horse for American power. The Norwegian government also applies for membership, and that application goes forward, until 1972.

1962: The European Social Fund and the Common Agricultural Policy are established.

1966: Without actually leaving NATO, De Gaulle expels NATO forces from France and withdraws French forces from joint command.

1967: General Agreement on Tariffs and Trade.

1967: Euratom, the ECSC, and the EEC are amalgamated into one European Community (EC) whose combined institutions of government are a Commission, a Council of Ministers, and a Parliament. Until 1979 Members of the European Parliament (MEPs) are chosen by their national governments.

1969: De Gaulle dies.

1970: Antonio Salazar, Portuguese dictator, dies.

1972: In a referendum, Norwegians vote against joining the EC.

1972: A terrorist attack at the Munich Olympics fuels interest in cooperation and closer political union.

1973: Britain, Denmark, and Ireland join the EC. Greenland, a Danish colony, is included.

1975: Francisco Franco, Spanish dictator, dies.

1979: For the first time, members of the European Parliament are directly elected by the citizens of their various nations. The EC establishes the European Monetary System, which attempts to stabilize the rates of exchange among member countries.

1981: Greece joins the EC.

1985: Greenland (now under home rule) withdraws from the EC in a quarrel over fishing regulations.

1985: A flag and wordless anthem are adopted by all member states, in addition to their own national symbols. May 9 is designated "Europe Day."

1986: Spain and Portugal, now democratically governed, join the EC.

1987: The Single European Act (SEA) comes into effect, preparing for a single market and greater institutional efficiency. It also enlarges EU commitments to scientific research, environmental policies, and aid for the poorer regions of the Union, and sets up procedures for a cooperative foreign policy.

1990s: Norway again applies to join the EC/EU.

1990: After long opposition, Prime Minister Margaret Thatcher agrees to tie the British pound to the EU's Exchange Rate Mechanism.

1990: As the Soviet Union dissolves, the two Germanys are reunited; EC membership is thus extended to the former East Germany.

1992: Economic stresses in the enlarged Germany affect other countries and lead to widespread devaluation; unable to shore up the pound, Britain leaves the ERM.

1992: Treaty of Maastricht, a year in the making, amends the Treaties of Rome to allow for new areas of intergovernmental cooperation, such as defense and justice, going beyond trade and finance. The EC becomes the EU. A timetable is adopted for economic and monetary union.

1993: The Single European Market removes all border barriers to the movement of people, goods, and services within the Union.

1994: By popular vote, Norwegians again reject membership, partly because of disagreements over the EU's position on whaling.

1994: The Anglo-French "Chunnel" built beneath the English Channel links Britain and Continental Europe.

1995: When the EU seems unable to respond to civil war and "ethnic cleansing" in Bosnia, NATO forces intervene.

1995: Austria, Finland, and Sweden join the EU, bringing total membership to 15.

1996: The EU bans British beef because of the danger of "mad cow" disease.

1997: The Treaty of Amsterdam consolidates the EU and EC treaties, and amends them slightly.

1999: The euro, a common currency, is adopted by 12 of the 15 member nations, at first only for financial institutions but by 2002 for all transactions, as national currencies are phased out. Britain, Denmark, and Sweden choose not to adopt the euro.

1999: NATO intervenes in Kosovo; European forces prove less effective than American forces.

2000: The EU plans a European Rapid Reaction Force.

2001: The Treaty of Nice is signed, bringing about additional consolidation. Changes in voting structure in the Council of Ministers give more power to smaller nations, especially Poland and Spain.

2002: In an unprecedented assertion of authority, the European Parliament forces the resignation of President August Sander and the European Commission on allegations of corruption. A new commission and a new commission president are appointed.

2003: A draft constitution is rejected, with disagreements over voting structure. The EU financial authority takes no disciplinary action against France or Germany, when those nations report deficits of more than 3 percent.

2003: EU forces join NATO peacekeepers in Macedonia; the EU undertakes an independent military deployment in the Congo.

2004: Ten more nations join the EU: the Baltic states of Estonia, Lithuania, and Latvia; the East European states of Poland, Hungary, the Czech Republic, Slovakia, and Slovenia; and the Mediterranean island states of Cyprus (the Greek part) and Malta.

October 27, 2004: Incoming Commission President José Barroso withdraws his proposed team of commissioners (the EU's executive) when he realizes that the European Parliament objects so strongly to one nominee that it will reject the entire panel. He assembles an alternative team the following month.

October 29, 2004: A revised constitution is signed by representatives of the member nations. However, 11 nations schedule referendums over the next few years for final approval.

December 2004: EU forces take over from NATO in Bosnia.

December 17, 2004: Turkey is invited to apply for membership in the European Union.

Bibliography

Books

Andonova, Liliana B. *Transnational Politics of the Environment: The European Union and Environmental Policy in Central and Eastern Europe.* Cambridge, Mass.: MIT Press, 2003.

Ash, Timothy Garton. *Free World: America, Europe, and the Surprising Future of the West.* New York: Random House, 2004.

Bomberg, Elizabeth, and Alexander Stubb. *The European Union: How Does It Work?* The New European Union Series. New York: Oxford University Press, 2003.

Cini, Michelle, ed. *European Union Politics.* New York: Oxford University Press, 2003.

Dinan, Desmond. *Europe Recast: A History of the European Union.* Boulder, Colo.: Lynne Rienner Publishers, 2004.

Dinan, Desmond. *Ever Closer Union: An Introduction to European Integration.* 2nd ed. Boulder, Colo.: Lynne Rienner Publishers, 1999.

Everts, Steven, et al. *A European Way of War.* London: Center for European Reform, 2004.

Gillingham, John. *European Integration 1950–2003: Superstate or New Market Economy?* New York: Cambridge University Press, 2003.

Gordon, Philip H., and Jeremy Shapiro. *Allies at War: America, Europe, and the Crisis over Iraq.* New York: McGraw-Hill, 2004.

McCormick, John. *Understanding the European Union: A Concise Introduction.* 2nd ed. New York: Palgrave, 2002.

Mester, Sándor. *The European Dream: The European Union for Outsiders.* Philadelphia: Xlibris, 2001.

Moravcsik, Andrew. *The Choice for Europe: Social Purpose and State Power from Messina to Maastricht.* Ithaca, N.Y.: Cornell University Press, 1998.

Neal, Larry, and Daniel Barbezat. *The Economics of the European Union and the Economies of Europe.* New York: Oxford University Press, 1998.

Nelsen, Brent F., and Alexander Stubb, eds. *The European Union: Readings on the Theory and Practice of European Integration.* 3rd ed. Boulder, Colo.: Lynne Rienner Publishers, 2003.

Nugent, Neill. *The Government and Politics of the European Union.* 5th ed. New York: Palgrave, 2002.

Peterson, John, and Elizabeth Bomberg. *Decision-Making in the European Union.* New York: St. Martin's Press, 1999.

Peterson, John, and Michael Shackleton. *The Institutions of the European Union.* New York: Oxford University Press, 2002.

Pinder, John. *The European Union: A Very Short Introduction.* New York: Oxford University Press, 2001.

Pond, Elizabeth. *Friendly Fire: The Near-Death of the Transatlantic Alliance.* Washington, D.C.: Brookings Institution Press, 2004.

Reid, T. R. *The United States of Europe: The New Superpower and the End of American Supremacy.* New York: Penguin Books, 2004.

Richardson, Jeremy John, ed. *European Union: Power and Policy-Making.* 2nd ed. New York: Routledge, 2001.

Rifkin, Jeremy. *The European Dream: How Europe's Vision of the Future Is Quietly Eclipsing the American Dream.* New York: Jeremy P. Tarcher Publishing, 2004.

Rosamond, Ben. *Theories of European Integration.* New York: Palgrave, 2000.

Sweet, Alec Stone, Wayne Sandholtz, and Neil Fligstein, eds. *The Institutionalization of Europe.* New York: Oxford University Press, 2001.

Wallace, Helen, and William Wallace. *Policy-Making in the European Union.* New York: Oxford University Press, 2000.

Web Sites

This section offers the reader the addresses of Web sites that can provide more extensive information on the European Union. These Web sites also include links to other sites that may be of help or interest. Due to the nature of the Internet, we cannot guarantee the continued existence of a site, but at the time of this book's publication, all of these Internet addresses were operational.

The European Union

europa.eu.int

This is the European Union's Web site. It offers extensive information on the Union itself and on its member countries, in 20 languages. Activities, institutions, documents, and services are covered.

Delegation of the European Commission to the United States

www.eurunion.org

This site provides information for Americans about the European Union and its role in current events, focusing especially on matters that affect relations between the EU and the United States.

EUobserver

www.euobserver.com

This is a privately run news service that is entirely concerned with the activities of the European Union and its various agencies. Articles are short, clear, and sometimes skeptical.

Additional Periodical Articles with Abstracts

More information on the European Union and related subjects can be found in the following articles. Readers who require a more comprehensive selection are advised to consult *Readers' Guide to Periodical Literature*, *Readers' Guide Abstracts*, *Social Sciences Abstracts*, and other Wilson publications.

Eastern Bloc Party. Jim Rosapepe. *American Prospect*, v. 15 pp14–15 July 20, 2004.

Rosapepe contends that the expansion of the European Union by 10 new members, of which the majority are Central and Eastern European former communist states that are also NATO countries, is giving the continent's economic dynamism a much-needed boost. On a visit to Bucharest, Romania, in Fall 2002, President George W. Bush attributed the "new" Europe's support for his policies on the wars on terrorism and in Iraq to "moral clarity," but in reality, the writer says, it was driven by those oldest of European diplomatic motivations: self-interest and realpolitik. The East Europeans intend to preserve their vital alliances with the U.S., but they are looking to a democratic and prosperous future, and that lies with the EU.

Euroconstitutional: British Opposition to EU Constitution. Jonathan Aitken. *American Spectator*, v. 37 pp48–49 September 2004.

In the author's opinion, Britain has begun a journey toward disengagement from the European Union. Until recently, Britain was a committed member of "Old Europe," to use Donald Rumsfeld's expression for the Franco-German–dominated EU, but Britain's commitment is weakening due to new political movements and developments, which are pushing the country into a radical reappraisal of its relationship with its Continental partners. The author gives Prime Minister Tony Blair credit for courage in his campaign for the new constitution, but believes it is a doomed endeavor.

Europe: Staring into the Abyss. Jeffrey E. Garten. *Business Week*, p24 August 2, 2004.

The author foresees a dismal future for Europe. The past decade has been one of lackluster growth and double-digit unemployment for the European continent, a situation he expects will continue. More fundamentally, Germany, France, and Italy, which together constitute more than 60 percent of activity in the euro zone, will be unable to compete with either the United States or China because they are stuck in an era in which it was an asset to have intimate banking relationships, permanent job security, and very high government financed entitlements. Meanwhile, the combination of Europe's aging populations, falling birthrates, and rising fiscal deficits makes America's problem of financing Social Security look easy. The result, the author believes, could be a gradual increase in European protectionism.

The Pernicious Rise of "Core Europe." John Rossant. *Business Week*, p57 May 10, 2004.

The author reports that some German and French policymakers are talking about "Core Europe," a narrow region revolving around France and Germany, with Spain, the Benelux countries, and perhaps eventually Italy playing supporting roles. Core Europe is distinct from the pro-American British, with their free-trade notions, and the poorer new EU members arriving from Central Europe. Core Europe's precepts are a sort of protectionism lite that uses market methods to promote the goals of a state-directed economy and keep U.S. influence in check, even if that means bending EU rules to advance the interests of the core.

Creating the Superstate. *Canada and the World Backgrounder*, v. 69 pp21–25 December 2003.

The article focuses on the EU's administrative center, the European Commission, claiming that it has developed a deservedly bad reputation. Although in theory the Commission works for the good of the entire community, in fact its bureaucrats—even at the top—have been accused of fraud, favoritism, extravagance, and mismanagement. In 1999 all 15 commissioners were forced to resign, resulting in a reevaluation of the role of the Commission and attempts to curtail its powers. The bureaucracy grinds on, however, generating an ever-increasing number of rules to bring conformity to every aspect of European civic life.

The Power of Unity. Rick Anderson. *Canada and the World Backgrounder*, v. 69 p3 December 2003.

According to the author, who works for the Toronto *Sunday Star*, modern Europe is a powerhouse economically, intellectually, politically, and diplomatically. Anderson contends, "European cities offer livable downtown cores, great public spaces, good transportation, and relatively low violent crime rates," compared to large North American cities. He praises the quality of life in Europe, as well as the richly varied political scene.

The Idea of Europe. Louis Dupre. *Commonweal*, v. 131 pp11–14 March 26, 2004.

Dupre reports that, in its efforts to write an appopriate introduction to a new European Union constitution, the committee preparing the document has triggered an unprecedented controversy over the spiritual identity of the Continent. This dispute was prompted by the absence of any mention of the historic role that Christianity played in educating and unifying the large numbers of tribes and countries that invaded Europe between the third and sixth centuries. Dupre argues that this unity of spirit in a variety of expressions must be remembered in forging the new European identity and should be referred to in the EU's constitution.

Idealism and Power: The New EU Security Strategy. Jean-Yves Haine. *Current History*, v. 103 pp107–12 March 2004.

Haine writes that the Iraqi crisis has led to significant progress in the creation of a common European security and defense policy. In 2003 profound divisions emerged over the war in Iraq, the abandoning of the stability pact that controls monetary union, the inability to reach agreement on an EU constitution, and the large amount of distrust and acrimoney evinced throughout the year. Nonetheless, according the Haine, the Iraqi crisis compelled the EU to acknowledge that a divided union has no strength. Consequently, it managed to divise and adopt the Union Security Strategy, the most ambitious security and defense initiative since the European Defense Community collapsed in August 1954.

After the Heat Wave: The Mud Flies. *Economist*, v. 368, p41 August 23, 2003.

The article discusses the political fallout the European authorities are facing from the summer's heat wave—the high body count has led to criticism of the health agencies' responses to the effects of soaring temperatures. The director of public health resigned in France, where the death toll, especially among the elderly and infirm, could be as high as 10,000; in Italy, the health minister has descended into a spate of bitter recriminations with local authorities; Spain also suffered unprecedented numbers of deaths, with the blame shifting between the central health ministry and the regional health services. In Portugal the issue was the mismanagement of firefighting against the lethal forest fires that ravaged the country.

The European Union: After Babel, a New Common Tongue. *Economist*, v. 372 pp41–42 August 7, 2002.

Over the centuries, Latin, German, French, and Russian have variously held linguistic sway in Europe, but in the 21st-century European Union, the new language of choice—rising up through the educational system and down from the business and political elite—is English. Three out of four secondary-school students in the EU member states and accession countries will study English; as a basic life skill, speaking English is on a par with the ability to drive a car or use a personal computer, and its dominance has been reinforced by the demands of foreign investors, who value a single language for business. It remains to be seen whether the EU's political integration will be accelerated by the generalized use of English.

Passport to Prosperity. *Economist*, v. 372 pp8–11 September 25, 2004.

One of the principal arguments for European unity—a reasonable expectation of ever-increasing prosperity—is being undermined by the now slow and intermittent nature of recent economic growth in western Europe, this article alleges. With efforts to stimulate the EU economy through bold reforms proving disappointing, European policymakers are glum. However, the trouble with the European social model of lower economic growth in return for more social protection and leisure time is not that it is illegitimate but that it is unsustainable, according to the article. Details of the menacing demographic time bomb that faces Europe, and its consequences for the EU, are provided.

Nuclear Power and EU Enlargement: The Case of Temelin. Regina Axelrod. *Environmental Politics*, v. 13 pp153–71 Spring 2004.

Axelrod discusses the controversy surrounding the impending commercial operation of the Temelin nuclear power plant in the Czech Republic in light of the country's accession to the EU. She outlines the development of the Temelin plant and the interactions between states, including how Temelin's proximity to Austria and the project's unique integration of Western and Russian technology serve as the basis for Austrian threats to veto Czech accession. She underscores the unusual role played by the EU as mediator in this controversy and nuclear power's role in the mix of energy resources as an issue in the accession talks.

End of French-Dominated Europe in Sight? Paul Johnson. *Forbes*, v. 173 p31 January 12, 2004.

The writer advises U.S. policy-makers to proceed on the long-term assumption that a European superstate, with a common foreign and military policy, will not emerge. The collapse of the constitution conference and discussions of a "two-tier" EU mean that unity has been abandoned. Johnson writes that the joint decision of the French and German governments to end the fiscal stability pact that underpins the common currency must, ultimately, spell the destruction of the euro as well.

Europe's Awkward Embrace. Cem Ozdemir. *Foreign Policy*, pp68–69 January/February 2004.

Conservative parties in Europe need to learn to embrace immigrants, Ozdemir writes, particularly the increasing Muslim population. Whereas America's Republicans and Democrats actively compete for the support of minorities, many of Europe's conservative parties are still skeptical of immigrants, complaining that they do not embrace European customs and traditions and obsessing over the so-called clash between Christianity and Islam. Nonetheless, Ozdemir argues, traditional conservative voters in Europe have much more in common with Muslims than either side would like to admit, and ethnic minorities will only grow as a potentially vital electoral force.

Europe's Quiet Leap Forward. Kenneth Rogoff. *Foreign Policy*, pp74–75 July/August 2004.

The author believes that the economic juggernaut that is the European Union may dominate the 21st century. The main reason that Europe's output per capita is only 70 percent of the United States' is that Europeans work fewer hours per week, take longer vacations, and retire earlier than Americans. According to Rogoff, when the Japanese, Americans, Chinese, and others start "consuming" more leisure over the next 50 years, Europe's relative economic size will expand. The region also has a remarkably well-educated and flexible workforce, even if it is hindered by dubious labor legislation, as in Germany. In addition, Rogoff writes, robust political and legal institutions drive economic growth, according to studies, and European institutions remain models of honesty and transparency compared with those in Asia, Latin America, and the Middle East.

Is Europe Too Cautious? Jordan Tama. *Foreign Policy*, pp88–90 January/February 2004.

According to Tama, Americans appear more willing than Europeans to utilize innovations that contain potential environmental or health risks. A collection of essays in the August/September 2003 issue of the French journal *Esprit* highlights the fact that the French and many other Europeans are inclined to be more prudent, using the "precautionary principle" to evaluate new technologies. This principle, Tama writes, has emerged as an ideological battlefield that is likely to have a negative effect on the resolution of scientific disputes and the health of trans-Atlantic ties. Policymakers in Europe and the United States may wish to apply the principle to the U.S.-European relationship.

The Transatlantic Relationship. Erik Jones, ed. *International Affairs*, v. 80 pp587–753 July 2004.

In this special issue on relations between the United States and Europe, topics include: rhetoric and reality; America as a European power; European security and defense policy after the invasion of Iraq; the Atlantic crisis of confidence; U.S. and EU goals for the wider Middle East; the identity of NATO; NATO and nuclear weapons; and transatlantic intelligence and security cooperation.

Anti-Frankenfood Movement Grows. Umut Newbury. *Mother Earth News*, p18 August/September 2004.

In this article about the controversy over genetically modified organisms (GMOs—crops or animals genetically altered by biotech firms looking to add desirable traits), Newbury writes that, because the long-term health and environmental effects of genetic engineering (GE) are unknown, many people are leery of firms adding so many GE ingredients to foods. In Europe, although the European Union recently approved the importation of genetically engineered corn, 22 countries have begun initiatives to ban GMOs, and hundreds of cities in Austria, Belgium, England, France, Germany, Greece, Ireland, Italy, and Slovenia have already passed GMO-free resolutions.

A High-Level Food Fight. William Greider. *Nation*, v. 277 p16 November 3, 2003.

According to Greider, a burgeoning conflict in globalization is pitting Europe against the United States in a battle over the cultural meaning of food. U.S. farmers have already embraced biotechnology and genetically modified (GM) crops. European consumers, however, having recently experienced the man-made catastrophe of mad-cow disease, are not prepared to accept the industry's standard assurances that GM food poses no threat to human health and safety or the environment. The European Union has devised what the author calls a fiendishly clever way of keeping GM produce out of Europe's food system without breaking the WTO's sacred principles of free trade: honest labeling. This approach causes massive problems for the expansionist plans of the biotech industry.

Reorienting Transatlantic Defense. Doug Bereuter. *National Interest*, pp75–83 Summer 2004.

In an examination of the future of NATO, the author explains that forecasts of the imminent demise of that organization are premature, as NATO is not a cold war institution seeking a new mission to keep itself alive but an indispensable tool for the democracies of the Euro-Atlantic region to ensure their security against the shared threats of global terrorism, proliferation of weapons of mass destruction, and the states that support such things.

California Crosses the Atlantic. Jack Thurston. *New Statesman*, v. 133 p11 August 30, 2004.

The writer reports that the new draft of the European Constitution contains a proposeal that could bring California-style direct democracy, embodying either republican idealism or mob rule, to Europe. The draft constitution contains a sentence stating that the EU Commission must put forward a policy proposal to the Council of Ministers if a million signatures in favor of the policy have been collected. This very mild form of direct democracy could have its advantages, because it would open the door for participatory democracy and solve the legitimacy problem that has plagued the EU.

How Much Does Europe Help the Palestinians? Shada Islam. *New Statesman*, v. 133 p33 July 12, 2004.

The author examines the extent of the financial support provided to the Palestinian cause by the European Union, for which peace in the Middle East has long been a strategic priority. EU aid covers humanitarian relief in general and, more controversially, provides for the construction of the institutions and infrastructure that will be needed by a future Palestinian state. The Palestinian Authority's efforts at reforming itself have been bolstered by EU funding, the author states.

Will Turkey Make It? Stephen Kinzer. *New York Review of Books*, v. 51 pp40–42 July 15, 2004.

Kinzer writes that, when they meet in December, the leaders of the EU nations are likely to vote to allow the start of negotiations that would lead to Turkey's joining the EU. Under the leadership of Recep Tayyip Erdogan, the country has entered a period of remarkably far-reaching change, Kinzer says. Since becoming prime minister in March 2003, he has pulled Turkey further toward democracy than it had moved in the previous 25 years. In addition, Europe's leader may give this Muslim country a "yes" vote because not doing so could be dangerous: Islamic fundamentalists already preach that Muslims must turn inward because the rest of the world wishes them harm.

Union, But Not Unanimity, as Europe's East Joins West. John Darnton. *New York Times* (late edition), ppA1+ March 11, 2004.

Darnton writes that when the European Union expands eastward in May 2004, it will end the 65-year divide caused by the 20th century's hot and cold wars and shift the Union from a plush club of 15 like-minded nations to a street bazaar of 25 countries, including eight strongly pro-American former Soviet satellites, differing in wealth, stature, and outlook. The writer explores the implications for the EU and the new member states.

Eurabia? Niall Ferguson. *New York Times Magazine*, pp13–14, April 4, 2004.

Muslim immigrants are filling Europe's population vacuum and reshaping the continent's culture, Ferguson writes. The United Nations forecasts that, even allowing for immigration, the population of the present European Union will drop by around 7.5 million over the next 45 years, and the aging of the population means choices will have to be made between high taxation, the abolition of retirement and health benefits, and more legal immigration. Immigrants will most likely come from neighboring countries, and Europe's fastest-growing neighbors are predominantly, if not entirely, Muslim. The writer considers possible outcomes for a future European culture.

How Not to Win Muslim Allies. Fareed Zakaria. *Newsweek*, v. 144 p39 September 27, 2004.

The author points out that Turkey has achieved the most dramatic economic, political, and social reforms of all developing countries over the past two years; nevertheless, it may not achieve its long-sought goal of full membership in the European Union. Many people in Europe want to keep Turkey out because it is large, poor, and Muslim, and recent events may have strengthened their hand. The Turkish parliament has insisted on introducing a law making adultery a criminal offense, and although the Turkish prime minister has opposed it and angrily stated that the issue of adultery is irrelevant to EU membership, the law provides a highly public issue to symbolize European fears.

Sovereignty and Democracy. Marc F. Plattner. *Policy Review*, pp3–17 December 2003/January 2004.

According to Plattner, the parallels drawn by American observers between the recent "European Convention" and the Philadelphia Convention of 1787 are extremely misleading. The European Convention, chaired by former French president Valery Giscard D'Estaing, has drafted a new EU constitution. Whereas the Philadelphia Convention was concerned about the correct locus of sovereignty and the appropriate scale of the state, in European scholarly and intellectual circles today the debate centers on whether the era of the modern state is ending. Many students and proponents of the EU seem to be moving toward the view that the EU can become a democratic non-state.

European Union Plans for Its Own CDC. Giselle Weiss. *Science*, v. 301 p581 August 1, 2003.

Weiss reports that the European Commission has approved a plan for a European Centre for Disease Prevention and Control (ECDC). Most officials previously favored a virtual network of centers for disease control rather than an actual physical center, but SARS, West Nile virus, and the recent anthrax scare have emphasized the importance of speed in dealing with public health threats. The ECDC, which must now be approved by the European Parliament, is intended to coordinate more effectively the responses of 15 national public health systems to emerging threats from communicable diseases.

Old Europe's New Ideas. Samuel Loewenberg. *Sierra*, v. 89 pp40–43, 50 January/February 2004.

By instructing industry to go green, the EU is challenging how America conducts business, says Loewenberg. In early 2001 American chemical executives heard that the EU was going to require manufacturers on both sides of the Atlantic to carry out extensive safety and environmental tests on 30,000 common chemicals, and of these, some 1,500 deemed the most dangerous would be severely restricted or banned. Until now, multinationals have primarily used their power and mobility to strong-arm governments into diluting environmental and labor regulations. Now, however, even with the European Commission's scaled-back draft of the legislation, U.S. companies will have to make greener products if they wish to sell them to Europe.

Not Such a Soft Power: The External Deployment of European Forces. Bastian Geigerich and William Wallace. *Survival*, v. 46 pp163–82 Summer 2004.

According to the authors, there were some real steps forward in various aspects of European defense cooperation in 2003, and in several countries taboos have been broken about the projection of military forces outside the EU. The writers believe that global demands on European forces are likely to grow, pushing European governments to seek to share limited resources within sharply constrained budgets. European governments collectively have doubled the number of troops deployed abroad within the past 10 years, with little national or Europe-wide debate, but a further rise in the demand for European forces, under circumstances that place them in harm's way, may bring debate out into the open.

What Unites Europeans? Gerard Baker. *Weekly Standard*, v. 9 pp17–18 July 26, 2004.

Baker reports that voters in Europe have been united in their angry reaction to the ambitious plans of the Continent's elite to accelerate and deepen a process of political integration that aims to create a superstate to rival the United States. As a result, according to Baker, there may be two Europes in existence within the next 10 years. One Europe would comprise a core group of countries that would be characterized by aging and sclerotic economies that are overregulated and overtaxed, as well as by exaggerated global ambitions to rival the United States as a superpower. The other Europe may comprise an outer eurozone of nations that will probably be strongly Atlanticist in outlook, promoting free markets and open trade and broadly supportive of U.S. global leadership. This latter group, writes Baker, is a Europe with which the United States would be happy to do business.

Europe a la Carte: Views of Liesbet Hooghe. *Wilson Quarterly*, v. 28 pp117–118 Winter 2004.

The writer discusses "Europe Divided? Elites vs. Public Opinion on European Integration," an article by Liesbet Hooghe that was published in the September 2003 issue of *European Union Politics*. Hooghe, a political scientist at the University of North Carolina, contends that the leaders of Europe and the citizens of Europe want very different things from the EU. She claims that although Europe's leaders want the EU to wield political muscle and govern a market that is sizable and competitive, its citizens would prefer the EU to be a caring entity that protects them from the vagaries of capitalist markets.

Europe's Identity Crisis. *World Press Review*, v. 50 pp21–26 September 2003.

In a special section on Europe, the writers included report that, as 10 new members join the EU, its recently created draft constitution has highlighted questions about the organization's reason for being. In the midst of new tensions across Europe, EU leaders must find agreement on the ties that connect them. Articles from newspapers from France, England, Poland, and Italy discuss various aspects of the issue.

Index

Adenauer, Konrad, 153
Afghanistan, 117
Africa and immigration, 100
agriculture
 bioengineered foods and, 148, 150
 farm subsidies, 37, 40, 79–80
 mad cow disease, 155
 policy trends, 7
Agriculture and Fisheries Council, 11
AIDS/HIV programs, 103, 121
Albrizio, Mauro, 148, 150
antitrust law, 86–87
Argentina, 147
Arie, Sophie, 99–100
asylum law, 97
Australia, 79, 102
Austria, 155

Barroso, José Manuel, 22–23, 114, 118, 127, 155
Barysch, Katinka, 65
Baykam, Zeki, 53
Beckmann, Andreas, 144
Belt, Don, 35–41
Berlin Plus, 114
Berlusconi, Silvio, 30, 100
Bermann, George, 84
bioengineered foods, 147–150
birth rates, 38, 97
Blair, Tony
 as Europhile, 25–27
 on U.S. relations, 123–124, 125–126
Bobinska, Lena Kolarska, 43
Bod, Péter Ákos, 64
Bonde, Jens-Peter, 24
border controls, 36, 39, 99–100, 121
Bosnia, 18, 114, 121, 155
Bowley, Graham, 22–24
Brand, Constant, 79–80
Bretton Woods exchange system, 70–72
Britain
 Euroskepticism in, 22–24, 25–26
 history, 27, 153–155
 Iraq War dissension and, 26, 125–128
 military operations, 115–116
 on U.S. relations, 118
 referendum on constitution, 26, 27
Brok, Elmar, 17
Bulgaria, 52, 71
bureaucracy, 42–43, 117
Burke, Maria, 143–146
Bush, George W., 119–120, 127, 129, 130, 138
Byrne, David, 103

Canada, 79, 102, 141, 147
Carter, Gina, 84, 87
Carter, Richard, 66–67
Center for European Reform (CER), 114
Charter of Fundamental Rights, 103–104
China, 148
Chirac, Jacques, 20, 123, 126–127
Clapp, Philip, 141
Collins, Erika Christian, 83, 87–88
Commission of the European Atomic
 Energy Community, 15
Commission of the European Economic
 Community, 15
Committee of the Regions, 5
community trademark, 84
Competitiveness Council, 11
conservatism, 25–26, 54–55
constitution, 25, 127
 adoption plans, 23
 as end of tripartite domination, 126, 127–128
 draft rejection, 27, 155
 referendum in Britain, 26
 religion in, 28–30
Corbett, Richard, 30
Council of the European Union, 5, 9, 10–12
Court of Auditors, 5
Court of Justice, 5
Crawford, Lester, 148

Crisis Centre, 111–112
Croatia, 18, 71
currency. *See* euro
Cyprus, 36–37, 145
Czech Republic, 39, 64, 97, 105–106, 143–
    145

Day After Tomorrow, The, 137–139
defense policy, 113–118, 120–121
    See also military operations
defense spending, 115
de Gaulle, Charles, 17, 153–154
Delors, Jacques, 17
Denmark, 94, 97–98, 154–155
Deppler, Michael, 68–78
Diamantopoulou, Anna, 38
Diringer, Elliot, 140–141
Dunleavy, Patrick, 27

Economic and Financial Affairs (Ecofin)
    Council, 11
Economic and Monetary Union (EMU),
    71, 73
economic reforms, 46, 63–65
economy. *See* finance
Education, Youth, and Culture Council
    (EYC), 12
elections, 10
    See also voting
employment law, 88
    See also labor and employment
environment
    bioengineered foods, 147–150
    EU expansion impact, 143–146
    fisheries, 154
    Kyoto Protocol, 127, 137–139, 140–
        142
    water/waste management, 144–145
Environment Council, 11
EPSCO (Employment, Social Policy,
    Health and Consumer Affairs Coun-
    cil), 11
Erdogan, Recep Tayyip, 54
Estonia, 38–41, 64, 97, 143–145
euro
    history, 8, 70–71, 155
    in Britain, 25
    requirements to adopt, 63–65
    transition to, 61–62
European Atomic Energy Community
    (EURATOM), 7, 9, 153

European Central Bank, 5, 63, 73
European Coal and Steel Community
    (ECSC), 6, 9, 15, 71, 153
European Commission, 5, 12–15, 85
European Economic and Social Commit-
    tee, 5
European Economic Community (EEC),
    7, 9, 70, 153
European Environment Agency (EEA),
    137–138
European Environment Bureau (EEB),
    146
European Investment Bank, 6
European Monetary System, 71, 154
European Ombudsman, 5
European Parliament, 5, 7, 9–10, 154
European Rapid Reaction Force, 155
European Union (EU)
    expansion of. *See* membership
    history and structure, 5–8, 9–16, 17–
        21, 81, 153–155
Europe Day, 154
Euroskepticism, 22–24, 25–26
Everts, Steven, 114, 116
exchange rate systems, 71–72, 154

Farmer, Andrew, 143–144
farmers, 39
farm subsidies, 37, 40, 79–80
finance
    defense spending, 115
    economic reforms, 46, 63–65
    EU-U.S. comparison, 73–76
    exchange rate systems, 71–72, 154
    income, per capita, 73, 76
    Lisbon Agenda, 66–67, 69–70
    price changes, 43
    social spending, 69–78, 96–98, 101–
        102
    taxation, 38, 51–52, 73
    welfare state vs. fiscal discipline, 68–
        78, 96
    See also euro; trade
Finland, 155
Fischer, Joschka, 125
Fischler, Franz, 79
fisheries, 154
    See also Agriculture and Fisheries
        Council
foods, bioengineered, 147–150
foreign policy, 119–121, 123–124, 125–

128
France
  anti-immigrant political parties, 94
  EU image in, 24
  fiscal deficit in, 64
  Iraq War dissension and, 125–128
  Muslim immigration to, 30
  on U.S. relations, 118, 123
  secularism, 28–29
Franco, Francisco, 154
Freedman, Lawrence, 114–115, 118
Funk, William, 84–85

Galileo system, 121
Garton Ash, Timothy, 17, 129–132
General Affairs and External Relations
    Council (GAERC), 11
genetically modified foods, 147–150
Germany, 131
  EU image in, 24
  fiscal deficit in, 64
  history, 154
  immigrants and, 99
  immigration to, 97–98
  Iraq War dissension and, 125–128
  on U.S. relations, 123
Gill, Lawrence, 82
global positioning systems, 121
global warming, 137–139, 140–142
  See also Kyoto Protocol
Goldsmith, Rebecca, 28–30
Golino, Louis, 113–118
Goodhart, David, 98
Grant, Charles, 114–115, 117–118
Greece, 154
Greenland, 154
Grybauskaite, Dalia, 42
Gyurcsány, Ferenc, 64, 123

Harding, Gareth, 137–139
Havel, Vaclav, 20
health services, 103–104, 105–106, 121
Heisbourg, François, 114
Helm, Tony, 123–124
High Authority, 7
HIV/AIDS programs, 103, 121
Holland, 94
homeland security, 36, 39, 111–112, 117,
    121
Hrobon, Pavel, 105

Hubner, Philipp, 149–150
human rights
  See also Charter of Fundamental
      Rights
Hungary, 37–39, 51–52, 64, 145

immigration
  illegal, 99–100
  impact of, 93–95
  of Muslims, 30
  public health resources and, 103–104,
      105–106
  refugees to Italy, 99–100
  social welfare benefits and, 96–98,
      101–102
income, per capita, 73, 76
India, 148
Iran, 121
Iraq, 117, 130–131
Iraq War, 26, 52, 115–116, 123, 125–128
Ireland, 154
Islamic immigrants. See Muslim immi-
    gration
Issing, Otmar, 63–64
Italy, 93, 99–100

Japan, 141
job creation, 67, 76
  See also labor and employment
Justice and Home Affairs Council (JHA),
    11

Kampfner, John, 50–52
Karas, Jacqueline, 144–145
Katz, Gregory, 25–27
Keohane, Daniel, 114, 116
Kohl, Helmut, 17
Koran, Nahit, 54–55
Kubinyi, Jozef, 105
Kyoto Protocol, 127, 137–139, 140–142

labor and employment
  employment law, 88
  job creation, 67, 76
  labor shortages, 93
  labor taxation, 72
  mobility restrictions, 51, 101
  physician workforce, 105–106
  policy reforms, 75–76
  unemployment rates, 47–48, 51, 102

Lamy, Pascal, 79–80
Landler, Mark, 63–65
Latvia, 143–144, 145
law
    administrative, 82–85
    antitrust, 86–87
    asylum/immigration, 97
    employment, 88
    See also European Court of Justice
Leadbetter, Jo, 80
Libya, 99–100
Lindert, Peter, 98
Lisbon Agenda, 66–67, 69–70
Lithuania, 42, 45–49, 97, 143–145
Lloyd, John, 94–95
Lomborg, Bjorn, 139

Machac, Pavel, 105
mad cow disease, 155
Madrid 2004 attacks, 111
Mahony, Honor, 111–112
Marcuss, Stanley, 83, 87
Marshall Plan, 153
Martins, Guilherme Oliveira, 62
Matonis, Audrius, 43
McGlade, Jacqueline, 137–139
McGuire, Stryker, 96–98
Meciar, Vladimír, 52
Meek, Colin, 103–104
membership
    countries, 2
    expansion of, 35–41, 42–44, 50–52,
        143–146
    Lithuania, 45–49
    Turkey, 19, 53–56, 71
Menon, Anand, 26–27
Microsoft Corp., 85
military operations, 18, 113–118, 121,
    155
    See also defense policy
Mitterrand, François, 17
Monnet, Jean, 7, 20, 153
Monsanto Corp., 147, 149
Moravcsik, Andrew, 119–121
Mozambique, 148
Muslim immigration, 30

Natapoff, Sam, 125–128
nationalism, 55
NATO (North Atlantic Treaty Organiza-
    tion), 50–52, 114, 116–117, 119–121,

153, 155
Neil, Martha, 81–88
NGOs (nongovernmental organizations),
    146
Niedermayer, Ludek, 64
Noreika, Pranas, 46–49
Norway, 153–154
Nowak, Stanislaw, 35, 40

O'Hanlon, Michael, 114–116
Oxfam, 80

Pastore, Ferruccio, 97
Payer, Markus, 148
Persson, Goran, 20
physician workforce, 105–106
Pim Fortuyn's List, 94
Poland, 28–29, 37, 43, 143–145, 155
Portugal, 154
Powell, Colin, 129
price changes, 43
public relations, 22–24
Putin, Vladimir, 50

Qaddafi, Muammar, 100
Qualified Majority Voting (QMV), 126
qualified majority voting (QMV), 12

Rachman, Gideon, 17–21
Ragusin, T. Andrew, 85–86, 88
refugees, 99–100
religious diversity, 28–30
Rice, Condoleezza, 130
Rifkind, Sir Malcolm, 25–26
Rising, David, 61–62
Romania, 52, 71
Rosenthal, Elisabeth, 147–150
Rowthorn, Bob, 94
Rucker, Martin, 45–49

Sachs, Susan, 53–56
Sacredeus, Lennart, 30
Salazar, Antonio, 154
Sandalow, David, 141
Sander, August, 155
Schreurs, Miranda, 143, 144
Schröder, Gerhard, 20, 126
Schuman, Robert, 5, 6, 20, 153
secularism, 28, 131
security, 36, 39, 111–112, 117, 121
Security and Growth Pact (SGP), 74
Shalgham, Mohammed Abdel-Rahman,
    100

Silina, Mara, 146
Single European Act (1986), 70, 154
single market, 8, 39, 43, 154
Slovakia, 51
social spending, 69–78, 96–98, 101–102
Solana, Javier, 114, 118, 121
Spain, 99–100, 111, 154, 155
Spotts, Peter, 140–142
Spritzer, Dinah, 105–106
Stability and Growth Pact (SGP), 71, 73, 78
Stephenson, Wen, 129–132
Stönner-Venkatarama, Oliver, 64
Svec, Ladilslav, 106
Sweden, 20, 96, 155
Swieboda, Pawel, 43
Switzerland, 147

taxation, 38, 51–52, 72
Taylor-Gooby, Peter, 98
terrorism, 52, 111–112, 117, 154
Thatcher, Margaret, 20, 154
Titford, Jeffrey, 22–24
trade, 8, 39, 43, 154
    See also exchange rate systems
Transport, Telecommunications, and
    Energy Council, 11
Treaties of Rome (1957), 7, 70, 153
Treaty of Amsterdam (1997), 155
Treaty of Maastricht (1992), 7, 71, 73, 154
Treaty of Nice (2003), 8, 12, 155
Treaty of Paris (1951), 153
Trichet, Jean-Claude, 63–64
Turco, Maurizio, 30
Turkey
    admission to EU, 19, 53–56, 71, 131, 155
    as U.S. ally, 127
    Muslim immigration and, 30

UK Independence Party (UKIP), 22
unemployment rates, 47–48, 51, 102
United Nations' Intergovernmental Panel

on Climate Change, 137
United States
    bioengineered foods, 147–149
    EU relations, 118, 119–121, 129–132
    farm subsidies, 79–80
    finance comparisons, 73–76
    foreign policy on, 119–121, 123–124, 125–128
    Kyoto Protocol and, 138
    military operations, 113–118
    religion in, 131
    social welfare benefits and, 96
    unilateralism and, 127, 129
    See also Iraq War

Verdun, Battle of, 17
Victor, David, 141–142
Vike-Freiberga, Vaira, 43
voter turnout, 22
voting, 12, 126, 155
    See also referendums

Wahl, Stephanie, 97
Wallstrom, Margot, 23–24
waste management, 144–145
water management, 144
Watson, Graham, 28–30
welfare state, 68–78, 96–98
Wermann, Chris, 149
Westin, Charles, 97
whaling, 154
Wilkison, Roger, 42–44
Winthrop, John, 132
Wittbrodt, Edmund, 29
World Trade Organization (WTO), 79–80

Yeltsin, Boris, 50
Younge, Gary, 98

Zambia, 148
Zoellick, Robert, 79–80

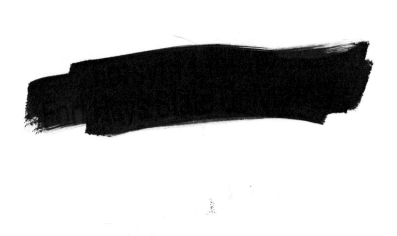